WITH CHRIST IN THE SCHOOL OF PRAYER

WITH CHRIST IN THE SCHOOL OF PRAYER

ANDREW MURRAY

REVISED BY
HAROLD J. CHADWICK

Bridge-Logos *Publishers*

North Brunswick, New Jersey 08902 USA

WITH CHRIST IN THE SCHOOL OF PRAYER
by Andrew Murray
Revised by Harold J. Chadwick
Copyright © 1999 by **Bridge-Logos** *Publishers*
Library of Congress Catalog Card Number: 99-90643
International Standard Book Number: 0-88270-779-5

Published by:
Bridge-Logos *Publishers*
1300 Airport Road, Suite E
North Brunswick, NJ 08902
http://www.bridgelogos.com

TABLE OF CONTENTS

PREFACE

Of all the promises connected with the command, "Abide in Me," there is none higher than this: "If you abide in Me, and My words abide in you, you will ask what you desire, and it shall be done for you."[1] Power with God is the highest attainment of the life of full abiding.

Of all the traits of a life like that of Jesus Christ, there is none higher and more glorious than conformity to Him in the work that now engages Him without ceasing in the Father's presence—His all-powerful intercession. The more we abide in Him and grow to be like Him, the more His priestly life will work in us. Our lives will become what His is—a life that continuously prays for people.

Christ has "made us kings and priests to our God."[2] Both a king and a priest possess power, influence, and blessing. The king's power goes downward. The priest's power rises upward, having power with God. In our blessed priest-king, Jesus Christ, the kingly power is founded on the priestly: "He is also able to save to the uttermost those who come to God through Him, since He always lives to make intercession for them."[3] In us, His priests and kings, it is no different. It is in intercession that the Church is to find and wield its highest power. In intercession, each member of the Church can prove their descent from Israel as a prince having power with God and with people.[4]

The place and power of prayer in the Christian life is too little understood. I feel sure that as long as we view prayer simply as the means of maintaining our own Christian lives, we will not fully understand what it is really supposed to be. But when we learn to regard it as the highest part of the work entrusted to us—the root and strength of all other work—we will see that there is nothing we need to study and practice more than the art of praying.

If I succeed in explaining the teaching of our Lord in regard to prayer, and succeed in pointing out the distinct reference that the wonderful promises of the Lord's last night have to the works we are to do in His name (the greater works,[5] and bearing much fruit,[6]), then we will all have to admit that it is only when the Church gives itself up to this holy work of intercession that we can expect the power of Christ to manifest itself on our behalf. It is my prayer that God may use this book to make clearer to some of His children the wonderful place of power and influence that He is saving for them. How the weary world awaits that show of power.

In connection with this, there is another truth that came to me with wonderful clarity as I studied the teachings of Jesus on prayer. *The Father waits to hear every prayer of faith. He wants to give us whatever we ask for in Jesus' name.* We have become so accustomed to limiting the wonderful love and the great promises of our God, that we cannot read the simplest and clearest statements of our Lord without qualifying them. If there is one thing I think the Church needs to learn, it is that God intends prayer to have an answer, and that we have not yet fully conceived of what God will do for us if we believe that our prayers will be heard. *God hears prayer.* This truth is universally admitted, but very few understand its meaning or experience its power.

If what I have written stirs you to go to the Master's words and take His wondrous promises simply and literally as they stand, my purpose has been attained.

There is an unspeakable blessing in learning how completely Christ is our life, and how He is and can do in us everything that we need. Have we learned yet to apply this truth to our prayer life? Many complain that they don't have the power to pray in faith an effective prayer that accomplishes much. The truth I want to reveal is that the blessed Christ is waiting and longing to teach us how to do this.

Christ is our life. In heaven He lives eternally to pray. His life in us is a life of continuous prayer, if we will simply trust Him for it. Christ teaches us to pray not only by example, by instruction, by command, and by promises, but by *showing us Himself, the eternal intercessor, as our life.* When we believe this, abiding in Him for our prayer life, our fears of not being able to pray right will vanish. We will joyfully and triumphantly trust our Lord not only to teach us to pray, but to become the life and the power of our prayer.

May God open our eyes to understand the holy ministry of intercession to which we have been set apart as His royal priests. May He give us a large and strong heart to believe what mighty influence our prayers can exert. And may all fear of our not being able to fulfill our vocation vanish as we see Christ living eternally to pray, living in us to pray, and guaranteeing the results of our prayer life.

Andrew Murray,
Wellington
October 28, 1885

Andrew Murray

House in which Andrew Murray was born, known as "the old Parsonage," which later became the home of his son, Charles.

View of Graaff-Reinet, (old church in background).

*Father and Mother of
Andrew Murray*

*Andrew
Murray as a
young minister*

*John Murray
as a
young minister*

*Andrew Murray
as a young student*

Marischal College, Aberdeen

The Murray Family in 1873. Andrew is in the back row with his arm affectionately around his wife.

The town of Andrew Murray's pastorate where great revival broke out, (1860-1864), Worcester, South Africa, about 1877.

1866 painting of Adderly Street, Cape Town, with the Dutch Reformed Church in the background.

*Andrew Murray's dwelling,
"Clairvaux" (on right) with the
Training Institute for
Missionaries (to the left).*

Professor Murray age 70

Andrew Murray (center) and his family about 1880.

Dr. Murray unveiling the Monument of his two colleagues, Professors J. Murray and N. Hofmeyr, 1915.

The beach house at Kalk Bay which Mr. Murray affectionately called "Patmos."

On the rocks at "Patmos," Andrew's favorite place of retreat.

Andrew Murray
in old age

BIOGRAPHY OF
ANDREW MURRAY

Andrew Murray was born in South Africa in 1828. His father and mother were missionaries with the Dutch Reformed Church. When he was ten, he and his older brother, John, were sent to Aberdeen, Scotland, to school. There they stayed with their father's brother, a well-known minister associated with the Free Church, and highly interested in revivals.

At that time, Scotland was experiencing a series of revivals along the order of those taking place in America during the Second Great Awakening (1795-1835) under Charles Grandison Finney. Because of their uncle's association with the Free Church and his interest in revivals, many of the great evangelists and preachers of that day were houseguests of the Murrays, and Andrew and his brother were enraptured by the many conversations on revival and the deeper life that took place during meals and in the evenings.

It was this close association with strong men and women of God, and intimate knowledge of what God was doing throughout Scotland and America, that convinced the boys to enter the ministry, much to the delight of their parents in South Africa. So in 1845 the Murray boys left Scotland for Holland to begin theological studies at the University of Utrecht. Andrew was now seventeen.

Although church life in Holland varied from lukewarm to dry—one professor at the university taught that there was no such things as miracles, that all could be explained by scientific or natural laws—John and Andrew found a fellowship that had formed a few years earlier at the university, and that was patterned after the discipleship societies of John Wesley. So much so, in fact, that some of the formalists scornfully referred to them as "a new sect of Methodists." It was this association with the *Zechar Debar* (Hebrew: "Remember the Word") fellowship that kept the Murrays steadfast and committed to the orthodox biblical theology they had received in South Africa and Scotland, even in the midst of the new rationalism and formalism that was rapidly invading the Holland church and the university.

In addition to the theological training that Andrew received at Utrecht, it was here that he had a great change he later referred to as his conversion—a definite experience by which he said he knew he more surely belonged to the Lord.

On May 9, 1848, after Andrew and John finished their university studies, the Hague Committee of the Dutch Reformed Church ordained them both. It was Andrew's twentieth birthday and he was the youngest candidate for the ministry ever ordained by that church. Shortly thereafter the brothers returned to South Africa to pastor churches.

At that time, all the appointments in the Dutch Reformed Church in South Africa were made by the British colonial governor. In keeping with social customs, John, being the oldest, was placed in charge of the church in the well-established and respected town of Burgersdorp. Andrew, being the youngest, was made pastor of the Dutch Reformed Church in the frontier town of Bloemfontein. His parish covered approximately 50,000 square miles that were sparsely inhabited by 15-25,000 Boers (Dutch colonists and intensely independent farmers). He was just twenty-one at the time, but he so impressed the Boers with his concern and earnest desire to help their families spiritually and educationally that he was an almost immediate success.

In 1854, Andrew was asked by church officials to travel to England to help with certain church businesses and to recruit pastors. At first he was reluctant to leave his parish for such a long trip and time, but his continual work building the church in Bloemfontein and traveling throughout his entire parish several times had left him in poor health, and so he decided to go in the hopes that his health would get better. But though he accomplished the church work, his health did not improve, and he was advised by the doctors in England that only extensive rest for several months would restore him to health. Of particular concern to him was pain in his arms and hands. Even a half-hour exertion would create intense pain, and the doctors could find no cure. He could not even write a note without the pain starting. It was pain that would stay with him throughout his life.

In March 1855, twenty-one months after he left South Africa, Andrew returned, stopping at Cape Town before returning to Bloemfontein. Although he planned to be there for only a few days, he was delayed when he stayed at the home of Mr. and Mrs. Rutherfoord and met their daughter, Emma. Before he left several weeks later, he proposed to her. And although she did not answer him immediately, after continued correspondence and several return trips, she accepted his proposal, and they were married in Cape Town on July 2, 1856. Andrew was twenty-eight and Emma was twenty-one.

Emma was the perfect Victorian wife, and a God-given complement and companion to her pastor/evangelist/writer husband. She was schooled in music, art, languages, widely read, and adept at managing a large and bustling household. Added to that she loved people, was spiritual and pious, and immediately set herself as a buffer between the many who had consumed so much of Andrew's time and health, leaving little for himself and for God. During the years of their marriage, Andrew and Emma had eight children that reached adulthood—four sons and four daughters.

Over the years, Emma also developed many personal ministries of her own, helping women and their families, starting prayer groups, even involving children in providing help and support for missionaries. She was also closely involved with her husband during the revival in Worcester, and in the battles he fought at Cape Town against the creeping liberalism in the Dutch Reformed Church in South Africa.

Emma was especially helpful with Andrew's writing, taking his dictations when he could not write himself because of the pain in his arms and hands. She also copied down many of his teachings that were given at the Keswick deeper life conventions in England and South Africa, and many of his seminar teachings—as can be seen in the wording in a number of his books. After she died, one of their daughters, Annie, became Andrew's secretary for the remaining years of his life, and faithfully recorded her father's notes and ideas and often filled them out into prose.

In 1860, the Murrays moved to Worcester, a smaller parish than Bloemfontein in which the Dutch farmers lived closer to each other and closer to town, all of which made it easier to pastor them. It was here in that same year that revival broke out in Andrew's church—a revival his father had prayed for for many years, and which Andrew immediately resisted because he thought it was nothing but emotionalism.

At every service he tried to quiet the loud and spontaneous praying that would grip almost every member of the congregation, often in the middle of his sermon. Then one evening he came down off the platform to again try to stop the boisterous praying, and a man approached and quietly said to him, "I think you are the minister of this congregation. Be careful what you do, for it is the Spirit of God that is at work here. I have just come from America and this is exactly what I witnessed there." That was enough for Andrew, and he immediately repented and became a champion of the revival. Over the next year and more, he traveled to Cape Town and surrounding areas and preached about what God was doing, and every place he went revival broke out.

In 1864, Andrew was made joint pastor of the large church in Cape Town, where he stayed for seven years. Then in 1871, he received a call from a smaller church in Wellington, about forty-five miles from Cape Town. To the surprise of almost everyone, he accepted the call and moved his family to the small town of 4,000 people. Without question, his almost constant ministry and travel for twenty-three years had weakened his health to the point where he felt a need to take a smaller work. Or perhaps it was God's will that all Andrew had experienced and learned now be put into writing.

From the parsonage in the small South African town of Wellington, Andrew Murray's ministry began to spread around the world as his spiritual experiences and knowledge were put into books and other writings on Church renewal, the deeper life, and revival. They flowed from him like a river—about 250 titles are now credited to him, with many of them translated into several languages. The titles of many of his books reflect his continual theme of a deeper life in Christ: *The True Vine, Abide in Christ, Absolute*

Surrender, The Prayer Life, The Lord's Table, How to Raise Your Children for Christ, With Christ in the School of Prayer, Be Perfect. Among the many books he wrote, there was also one on healing, based upon his own experience and consequent studies.

In 1879-80, Andrew Murray literally lost his voice. He could barely talk above a whisper, and preaching was impossible, especially the fiery and lengthy sermons that were his custom. His throat had given out, put itself into a "relaxed condition," and would not come out of it. It looked as though Andrew's preaching days were over. Although he tried rest and treatment, except for a brief respite in late 1881, nothing worked. In the hopes that rest and a change of climate would cure their pastor, the Wellington church board suggested he take an extended trip to Europe, where he could also consult with more experienced doctors. So in May 1882, Andrew and Emma boarded a ship for London.

Not long after arriving in London, Andrew coincidentally met a Pastor Stockmaier who had written several books on healing through prayer that Andrew had read some years before. He and Emma had planned to travel to Switzerland, where Stockmaier lived, to meet with him, but here he was in London at the same time they were. Over the next few weeks, Stockmaier met with Andrew several times and gradually corrected many common Christian misconceptions he had about suffering and healing. Toward the end of that time, Andrew discovered a residential healing center in London called Bethshan and he and Emma made arrangements to study and pray there until he was healed. Not long after they moved in, Andrew went to the altar during a service, was anointed with oil, and his throat was instantly—and permanently—healed. He and Emma returned to Africa in October 1882.

In 1884, Andrew wrote and published a book titled: *Divine Healing.* From a publishing standpoint, it was an instant success, but from a church standpoint it was a disaster. In almost every Dutch Reformed Church in South Africa, congregation members asked their pastors to anoint them with oil and pray the prayer of faith over them so that they would be healed of their afflictions. If one of their leading pastors in South Africa could be healed by faith, why could they not be? But almost without exception the pastors had no belief in healing or faith for it, and they protested so strongly to the Dutch Reformed Church leaders that Andrew was forced—or agreed—to withdraw the book from publication. Even today the book is seldom published.

During the remainder of his life, Andrew Murray traveled to several countries to proclaim the gospel of Jesus Christ and the deeper life in Him. Often he preached at the Keswick (Deeper Life, Holiness) Conventions in England and South Africa, preached with Moody and Sankey during their last evangelistic tour in England, and traveled to the United States and preached in Moody's school in Northfield, Massachusetts, and also in several other places.

On January 2, 1905, at the age of seventy, Emma died from a stroke. A year later Andrew retired from the pastorate, but remained active in writing, speaking, and traveling, gradually decreasing his circle of travel until he seldom ventured far from Wellington. He died there on January 18, 1917, four months short of his eighty-ninth birthday.

Although dead, Andrew Murray's ministry continues to live in the multitude of books he has written, such as this one, *With Christ in the School of Prayer*, which he wrote three years after his healing. Each of his books is intended to lead the reader deeper into Christ, into that inner Holy of Holies where only the hungry venture, and where only the sanctified stay. It is the place where Christ stands and beckons to each of us, "Come all you who are weary and heavy laden . . ." It is the place where Andrew Murray went, and where he urges us to follow him and all those that A. W. Tozer once referred to as "the saints of the burning hearts."

Harold J. Chadwick

Prologue

The Only Teacher

One day Jesus was praying in a certain place. When He finished, one of His disciples said to Him, "Lord, teach us to pray, just as John taught his disciples." [1]

The disciples had learned to understand something of the connection between Jesus' wondrous life in public and His secret life of prayer. They had been with Him and had seen Him pray. They had learned to believe in Him as a Master in the art of prayer. None could pray like Him. So they went to Him with the request, "Lord, teach us to pray." In later years they would undoubtedly tell others that there were few things more wonderful or blessed that He taught them than His lessons on prayer.

It is still true today that disciples who truly see Him, feel the need of repeating the same request, "Lord, teach us to pray." As we grow in the Christian life, the thought and the faith of our beloved Master in His unfailing intercession become more precious, and the hope of being like Christ in His intercession gains an attractiveness never before known. As we see Him pray, and remember that there is none who can pray or teach like Him, we feel that the petition of the disciples, "Lord, teach us to pray," is just what we need. Everything He is and has is our very own. Because Christ Himself is our life, we can be certain that if we ask He will be delighted to take us into closer fellowship with Him and teach us to pray as He prays.

GO TO THE MASTER

Go to the Blessed Master and ask Him to enroll your name in the school that He always keeps open for those who long to study the divine art of prayer and intercession.

Yes, let us say to the Master as they did of old, "Lord, teach us to pray." Having done so, we will soon find that as we meditate on our prayer each word of our petition is full of meaning.

LORD, TEACH US *TO PRAY*

Yes, *to pray*. This is what we need to be taught. Though in its beginnings prayer is so simple that the feeblest child can pray, it is at the same time the highest and holiest work to which we can rise. Prayer is fellowship with the Unseen and Most Holy One. The powers of the eternal world have been placed at prayer's disposal. It is the very essence of true religion and the channel of all blessings. It is the secret of power and life not only for ourselves, but for others, for the Church, and for the world. It is to prayer that God has given the right to take hold of Him and His strength. It is on prayer that the promises wait for their fulfillment, the kingdom waits for its coming, and the glory of God waits for its full revelation. How slothful and unfit we are for this blessed work.

Only the Spirit of God can enable us to do it right. How speedily we are deceived into resting in a form of prayer, while the power is still missing. Our early training, the teaching of the Church, the influence of habit, the stirring of the emotions—how easily these lead to prayer that has no spiritual power and achieves little. Who would not cry out for someone to teach them true prayer that takes hold of God's strength and achieves much, to which the gates of heaven are really opened wide?

Jesus has opened a school in which He trains those of His redeemed ones who especially desire to have power in prayer. Enter it with the petition, "Lord, this is just what we need to be taught. O teach us *to pray.*"

LORD, TEACH *US* TO PRAY

Yes, *us*, Lord. We have read in Your Word about the power Your believing people of long ago had when they prayed, and what mighty wonders were done in answer to their prayers. This took place under the Old Covenant, in the time of preparation. Now, in these days of fulfillment, how much more will You give Your people a sure sign of Your presence?

We have heard the promises given to Your apostles of the power of prayer in Your name, and have seen how gloriously they experienced the truth of those promises. We know for certain they can become true to us, too. We hear continually, even in these days, what glorious tokens of Your power You still give to those who trust You completely, Lord. Teach us to pray with power, too.

The promises are for us, and the powers and gifts of the heavenly world are for us. O teach us to pray so that we may receive abundantly. To us, too, You have entrusted Your work. On our prayer, too, the coming of Your kingdom depends. In our prayer, too, You can glorify Your name. "Lord, teach *us* to pray." We offer ourselves as learners. We want only *You* to teach us.

LORD, *TEACH* US TO PRAY

Yes, we feel the need now of being *taught* to pray. At first there is no work that appears so simple, and later there is none that is more difficult. Then the confession is forced from us: "We do not know how to pray as we should."[2] It is true we have God's Word with its clear and sure promises, but sin has so darkened our mind that we don't always know how to apply the Word. In spiritual matters we do not always seek the most important things. In temporal matters we are still less able to use the wonderful liberty our Father has given us to ask for what we need.

Even when we know what to ask for, so much is still needed to make prayer acceptable. It must be to the glory of God, in full surrender to His will, in full assurance of faith, in the name of Jesus Christ, and with a perseverance that, if need be, refuses to be denied. All this must be learned. It can only be learned in the school of much prayer, for only practice makes perfect.

Amid the painful consciousness of ignorance and unworthiness, in the struggle between believing and doubting, the heavenly art of effective prayer is learned. There is one—the author and perfecter of faith[3] and prayer—who watches over our praying and sees to it that in all who *trust Him for it,* education in the school of prayer is carried on to perfection. Let the deep undertone of all our prayers be the teachableness that comes from faith in

Him as a perfect teacher, and we can be sure that we will be taught. We will learn to pray in power. Yes, we can depend on His teaching us to pray.

LORD, TEACH US TO PRAY

No one can teach like Christ. A pupil needs a teacher who knows his work, who has the gift of teaching, who in patience and love will descend to the pupil's needs. Blessed be God! Christ is all this and much more. It is Christ, praying Himself, who teaches us to pray. He knows what prayer is. He learned it amid the trials and tears of His earthly life. In heaven it is still His beloved work. His life there is prayer. Nothing delights Him more than to find those whom He can take with Him into the Father's presence, clothing them with power to pray down God's blessing to those around them, training them to work with Him in the intercession by which the kingdom is to be revealed on earth.

Christ knows how to teach, whether it is by the urgency of perceived need, by the confidence that joy inspires, by the studying of the Word, or by the testimony of another believer who knows what it is to have prayer heard. By His Holy Spirit He has access to our hearts and teaches us to pray by showing us the sin that hinders the prayer, or by giving us the assurance that we please God. He teaches by giving not only thoughts of what to ask or how to ask, but by breathing into us the very spirit of prayer and living within us as the great intercessor. We can most joyfully say, "Who teaches like Him?"

Jesus never taught His disciples how to preach, only how to pray. To know how to speak to God is more than knowing how to speak to people. Power with God is the first thing, not power with people. Christ loves to teach us how to pray.

A 30-DAY COURSE ON PRAYER

What do you think, beloved disciple of Christ? Isn't it just what we need to ask the Lord for, *a 30-day course of special lessons on the art of prayer?*

As we meditate on the words Jesus spoke on earth, let us yield ourselves to His teaching in the fullest confidence that with such a teacher, we will make progress. Let us take time not only to meditate, but to pray, to sit at the foot of the throne and be trained for the work of intercession. Let us do so in the assurance that despite our stammerings and fears, He is carrying on His work most beautifully. He will breathe His own life of prayer into us. As He makes us partakers of His righteousness and His life, He will make us partakers of His intercession, too.

As the members of His Body, as a holy and royal priesthood,[4] we will take part in His priestly work of praying to and getting results from God for humanity. Yes, even though we are unknowing and weak, let us most joyfully say, "Lord, teach us to pray."

LORD, TEACH US TO PRAY

Blessed Lord! You live eternally to pray, and can teach me, too, to live eternally to pray. You want me to share Your glory in heaven by sharing this unceasing prayer with You, standing as a priest in the presence of my God.

Lord Jesus! Enroll my name among those who

confess that they don't know how to pray as they should, and who especially ask You for a course of teaching in prayer.

Lord! Teach me to be patient in Your school, so that You will have time to train me. I am ignorant of the wonderful privilege and power of prayer, of the need for the Holy Spirit to be the spirit of prayer. Lead me to forget my thoughts of what I think I know, and make me kneel before You in true teachableness and poverty of spirit.

Fill me, Lord, with the confidence that with You for my teacher, I will learn to pray. Then I will not be afraid, because You pray continuously to the Father, and by Your prayer rule the destinies of Your Church and the world. Unfold for me everything I need to know about the mysteries of the prayer-world. When there is something I may not understand, teach me to be strong in faith, giving glory to God.

Blessed Lord! I know that You won't put a student to shame who trusts You. And, with Your grace, this student won't shame You, either. Amen.

Notes on the Prologue

[1] Luke 11:1
[2] Romans 8:26
[3] Hebrews 12:2
[4] 1 Peter 2:5, 9

LESSON 1

THE TRUE WORSHIPPERS

*"Yet a time is coming and has now come
when the true worshipers will worship the
Father in spirit and truth, for they are the
kind of worshipers the Father seeks.
God is spirit, and His worshipers must
worship in spirit and in truth."*[1]

These words of Jesus to the woman of Samaria are
His first recorded teaching on the subject of prayer.
They give us some wonderful first glimpses into the
world of prayer. The Father *seeks* worshippers. Our
worship satisfies His loving heart and is a joy to Him.
He seeks *true worshippers* but finds many who are not
the way He would like them. True worship is that which
is *in spirit and truth.* The Son has come to open the
way for this worship in spirit and in truth, and to teach
it to us. One of our first lessons in the school of prayer
must be to understand what it is to pray in spirit and in
truth and to know how we can attain it.

1

To the woman of Samaria our Lord spoke of a threefold worship:

1. The ignorant worship of the Samaritans: "You Samaritans worship what you do not know"[2]
2. The intelligent worship of the Jew, having the true knowledge of God: "We worship what we do know, for salvation is from the Jews"[3]
3. The new, spiritual worship which He himself has come to introduce: "Yet a time is coming and has now come when the true worshipers will worship the Father in spirit and truth"[4]

IN SPIRIT AND IN TRUTH

The words "in spirit and truth" do not mean earnestly, from the heart, or in sincerity. The Samaritans had the five books of Moses and some knowledge of God. There was doubtless more than one among them who honestly and earnestly sought God in prayer. The Jews had the true, full, revelation of God in that portion of His Word that had been given. There were godly people among them who called on God with their whole hearts, but not "in spirit and truth" in the full meaning of the words. Jesus said, *a time is coming and has now come.* Only in and through Him will the worship of God be in spirit and truth.

Among Christians, one still finds the three classes of worshipers. Some in their ignorance hardly know what they're asking for. They pray earnestly, but receive little. There are others having more correct knowledge who try to pray with all their minds and hearts. They often pray most earnestly and yet do not attain the full blessedness of worship in spirit and truth. It is into the third class we must ask our Lord Jesus to take us. He must teach us how to worship in spirit and truth. This alone is spiritual worship—this makes us the kind of worshipers the Father seeks. In prayer, everything will depend on our understanding and practicing worship in spirit and truth.

HARMONY BETWEEN GOD AND HIS WORSHIPPERS

The first thought suggested here by the Master is that there must be harmony between God and His worshipers. This is according to a principle that prevails throughout the universe—correspondence between an object and the organ to which it reveals or yields itself. The eye is receptive to light, the ear to sound. The person who truly wants to worship God—to find, know, possess, and enjoy God—must be in harmony with Him and have the capacity for receiving Him. Because God *is spirit,* we must worship *in spirit.*

What does this mean? The woman had asked our Lord whether Samaria or Jerusalem was the true place of worship. He answers that henceforth worship is no longer to be limited to a certain place: "Believe me, woman, a time is coming when you will worship the Father neither on this mountain nor in Jerusalem."[5] God is spirit, not bound by space or time. In His infinite perfection, He is the same always and everywhere. His worship must not be confined by place or form, but be spiritual as God himself is spiritual.

This is a lesson of deep importance. How much our Christianity suffers from being confined to certain times and places. Those who seek to pray earnestly only in the church building or in the prayer closet spend the greater part of their time in a spirit that is totally different from that in which they seek to pray. Their worship is the work of a fixed place or hour, not of their whole being. God is spirit. What He is, He is always and in truth. Our worship must be the same—*it must be the spirit of our life.*

WORSHIP IN THE SPIRIT MUST COME FROM GOD

The second thought that comes to us is that this worship in the spirit must come from God Himself. Because God is spirit, He alone has the Spirit to give. He sent His Son to fit us for such spiritual worship by giving us the Holy Spirit. It is of His own work that Jesus speaks when He says twice, *"a time is coming,"*[6] and then adds, *"and has now come."*

Jesus came to baptize with the Holy Spirit, who could not stream forth until Jesus was glorified.[7] When Jesus had made an end of sin, He entered into the Holiest of All with His blood.[8] There on our behalf He *received* the Holy Spirit[9] and sent Him down to us as the Spirit of the Father. It was when Christ had redeemed us and we had received the position of children that the Father sent the Spirit of His Son into our hearts to cry, "Abba, Father."[10] The worship in spirit is the worship of the Father in the Spirit of Christ, the Spirit of sonship.[11]

This is the reason why Jesus uses the name of Father here. We never find one of the Old Testament saints personally appropriating the name of child in relation to God or calling God their Father. The worship

4

of *the Father is* only possible for those to whom the Spirit of the Son has been given. The worship *in spirit* is only possible for those to whom the Son has revealed the Father, and who have received the spirit of sonship. It is only Christ who opens the way and teaches the worship in spirit.

WORSHIP IN SPIRIT AND *IN TRUTH*

In truth does not only mean *in sincerity.* Nor does it only signify accordance with the truth of God's Word. The expression is one of deep and divine meaning. Jesus is "the only begotten of the Father, full of grace and *truth.* "[12] "The law was given through Moses; grace and *truth came* through Jesus Christ."[13] Jesus said, " "*I am* . . . *the truth* and the life."[14] The Old Testament was all shadow and promise. Jesus brought and gives the reality, *the substance* of things hoped for.[15] In Him the blessings and powers of the eternal life are our actual possession and experience.

THE SPIRIT OF TRUTH.

The Holy Spirit is the Spirit of truth, through whom the grace that is in Jesus[16] is ours, a positive communication out of His divine life. Thus worship in spirit is worship *in truth.* This actual living fellowship with God is a real correspondence and harmony between the Father who is spirit and the child praying in the spirit.

The woman of Samaria could not immediately understand what Jesus said to her. Pentecost was needed to reveal its full meaning. We are inadequately prepared to grasp such teaching at our first entrance into the school of prayer. We will understand it better later on.

Let us begin by taking the lesson as He gives it. *We are carnal and cannot bring God the worship He seeks.*

But Jesus has given us the Spirit. Let our attitude in prayer be what Jesus' words have taught us. Let there be the deep confession of our inability to bring God the worship that is pleasing to Him, the childlike teachableness that waits for Him to instruct us, and the simple faith that yields itself to the breathing of the Spirit. Above all, let us hold on tightly to this blessed reality—the secret of prayer in spirit and truth is in the knowledge of the Fatherhood of God, the revelation of His infinite fatherliness in our hearts, and the faith in His infinite love for us as His children. This is the new and living way Christ opened for us. To have Christ the Son, and *the Spirit of the Son,* dwelling with us and revealing the Father, makes us true, spiritual, worshipers.

LORD, TEACH US TO PRAY

Blessed Lord! I adore the love with which You taught the Samaritan woman at Jacob's well what the worship of God must be. [17] *I rejoice in the assurance that You will instruct with the same love any disciple who comes to You with a heart that longs to pray in spirit and truth.*

O my Holy Master! Teach me this blessed secret.

Teach me that worship in spirit and truth is not anything from us, but comes only from You. It is not only a thing of times and seasons, but the outflowing of a life in You. Teach me to get near to God in prayer with the attitude that I am ignorant and have nothing in myself to offer Him. But, at the same time, remind me of the provision that You, my Savior, make for the Spirit's breathing in my childlike stammerings.

I bless You because in You I am a child, and I have a child's liberty of access to the Father. In You I have the spirit of sonship and of worship in truth.

Teach me above all, blessed Son of the Father, the revelation of the Father that gives confidence in prayer. Let the infinite fatherliness of God's heart be my joy and strength for a life of prayer and of worship. Amen.

NOTES ON LESSON ONE

[1] John 4:23-24

[2] John 4:22

[3] Ibid.

[4] John 4:23

[5] John 4:21

[6] John 4:21, 23

[7] John 1:33, 7:37-38, 16:7

[8] Hebrews 9:12

[9] Acts 2:33

[10] Galatians 4:6

[11] Romans 8:15 (see NIV)

[12] John 1:14

[13] John 1:17

[14] John 14:6

[15] Hebrews 11:1

[16] John 1:14-17

[17] John 4:6-24

PERSONAL NOTES

_____

_____

_____

_____

_____

_____

_____

_____

_____

_____

_____

_____

_____

LESSON 2

ALONE WITH GOD

*"But when you pray, go into your room,
close the door and pray to your Father,
who is unseen. Then your Father, who sees
what is done in secret, will reward you."[1]*

After Jesus had called His first disciples, He gave
them their first public teaching in the Sermon on the
Mount.[2] There He explained the kingdom of God—its
laws and its life—to them. In that kingdom, God is not
only king, but Father, He not only gives all, but is
Himself all. The knowledge and fellowship of God alone
is blessedness. Hence it came as a matter of course that
the revelation of prayer and the prayer life was a part of
His teaching concerning the new kingdom He came to
establish. Moses gave neither command nor regulation
with regard to prayer. Even the prophets said little about
prayer. It is Christ who teaches us to pray.

9

A Secret Place for Prayer

The first thing the Lord taught His disciples is that they must have a secret place for prayer. Everyone must have some solitary spot where they can be alone with God. Every teacher must have a schoolroom. We have learned to know and accept Jesus as our only teacher in the school of prayer. He has already taught us at Samaria that worship is no longer confined to specific times and places. Worship—true spiritual worship—is a thing of the spirit and the life. A person's whole life must be worship in spirit and truth.

But Jesus wants each of us to choose for ourselves a fixed spot where we can meet Him daily. That inner chamber, that solitary place, is Jesus' schoolroom. That spot can be anywhere. It can even change from day to day if we're traveling. But that secret place must be somewhere with quiet time for the pupil to be in the Master's presence. Jesus comes there to prepare us to worship the Father.

Teachers always want the schoolroom to be bright, attractive, and filled with the light and air of heaven. They want it to be a place where their pupils long to come and love to stay. In His first words on prayer in the Sermon on the Mount, Jesus seeks to set the inner chamber before us in its most attractive light. If we listen carefully, our main purpose in being there becomes obvious. Jesus uses the name of Father three times: "pray to *your Father*," "*your Father* . . . will reward you," "*your Father* knows what you need."[3]

FIRST THING IN CLOSET PRAYING

The first thing in closet praying is to meet the Father. The light that shines in the closet must be the heavenly light that comes from the Father.⁴ The atmosphere in which we breathe and pray is God's love as our Father, His infinite fatherliness. Thus, each thought or petition we breathe out will be in simple, hearty, and childlike trust in the Father.

The Master teaches us to pray by bringing us into the Father's living presence. What we pray there must be of value. We should listen carefully to hear what the Lord has to say to us.

PRAY TO YOUR FATHER, WHO IS UNSEEN

God is an unseen God and hides Himself to the carnal eye. As long as in our worship of God we are chiefly occupied with our own thoughts and exercises, we will not meet Him who is spirit, the unseen one. But to those who withdraw themselves from all that is of the world and people, and wait for God alone, the Father will reveal Himself. As we shut out the world and its life, surrendering ourselves to be led by Christ into God's presence, the light of the Father's love will fall on us.

The secrecy of the inner chamber and the closed door, the entire separation from everything around us, is an image of the inner spiritual sanctuary, the secret of God's tabernacle. It is there within the veil that our spirit truly comes into contact with the invisible one.⁵

Thus we are taught at the very beginning of our search for the secret of effective prayer to remember that it is in the inner chamber, where we are alone with the Father, that we learn to pray properly. The Father is unseen, in secret. In these words, Jesus teaches us where He is waiting for us and where He is always to be found.

Christians often complain that their private prayer is not what it should be. They feel weak and sinful, and their hearts are cold and dark. It is as if they have no faith or joy in what little they have to pray about. They are discouraged and kept from prayer by the thought that they cannot come to the Father as they should or as they wish.

The Father Is Waiting for You

Listen to your Teacher. He tells you that when you go to private prayer your first thought must be that the Father is waiting for you there in secret—waiting unseen. Don't let a cold and prayerless heart keep you from the presence of the loving Father.

The Lord is concerned about you the way a father and mother are concerned about their children. Do not think about how little you have to give to God, but about how much He wants to give to you. Just place yourself before His face and look up into it. Think of His wonderful, tender, concerned love. Tell Him how sinful, cold, and dark everything is. The Father's loving heart will give light and warmth to yours.

Do what Jesus says. Just shut the door and pray to the Father in secret. Isn't it wonderful to be able to go alone to the infinite God? Just look up and say, "My Father."

YOUR FATHER WILL REWARD YOU

Jesus assures us that secret prayer cannot be fruitless, it will be rewarded, and its blessings will be evident in our lives. All we have to do is entrust our lives on earth to God when we are in secret and alone with Him. He will reward us openly and see that the answer to our prayer is made manifest in His blessing upon us. Our Lord teaches us that because God meets us in secret with infinite fatherliness and faithfulness, we should meet Him with childlike simplicity of faith and be confident that our prayer will receive a blessing. "Anyone who comes to God must believe that *He . . . rewards those who earnestly seek him.*"

The blessing of the closet does not depend on the strong or fervent feeling with which I pray, but on the love and power of the Father to whom I there entrust my needs. Remember your Father sees and hears in secret. Go there and stay there, then leave in confidence. God will answer. Trust Him and depend on Him for it. Prayer to the Father cannot be in vain. He will reward you openly.

YOUR FATHER KNOWS WHAT YOU NEED

Jesus said, "Your Father knows what you need before you ask him." By this the Lord further confirms faith in the Father-love of God. At first sight it might appear as if this thought made prayer less necessary— God knows what we need far better than we do. But as we get a deeper insight into what prayer really is, this truth will help to strengthen our faith. It will teach us that we do not need to compel an unwilling God to listen to us with the multitude and urgency of our words. It will lead to a holy thoughtfulness and silence in prayer as it suggests the question: *Does my Father really know that I need this?*

Once we have been led by the Spirit to the certainty that our request is indeed something that, according to the Word, we need for God's glory, we will have the wonderful confidence to say, "My Father knows I need it and must have it." If there is any delay in the answer, we will learn to hold on in quiet perseverance.

SIMPLICITY OF A CHILD

Christ your teacher would like to cultivate the blessed liberty and simplicity of a child in you as you draw near to God. *Look up to the Father until His Spirit works it in you.*

Sometimes in our prayers we are so occupied with our fervent, urgent, petitions that we forget that the Father knows and hears. At those times just hold still and quietly say, "My Father sees, my Father hears, my Father knows." It will help your faith to take the answer and say, "I know that I have what I asked of him."[6]

PRACTICE PRAYING

Now that you have entered the school of Christ to be taught to pray, take these lessons, practice them, and trust Him to perfect you in them. Go to the inner chamber often. Close the door so that you are shut off from people and shut up with God. There the Father waits for you, and there Christ will teach you to pray.

To be alone in secret with the Father should be your highest joy. To be assured that the Father will

14

openly reward your secret prayer so that it cannot remain unblessed should be your strength day by day. And to know that the Father knows that you need what you ask should be your liberty to bring every need to Him in the assurance that He will supply it according to His riches in glory in Christ Jesus.[7]

LORD, TEACH US TO PRAY

Blessed Savior! With my whole heart I bless You for designating the inner chamber as the school where You meet each of your pupils alone to reveal the Father to them.

O my Lord! Strengthen my faith in the Father's tender love and kindness, so that when I feel sinful or troubled, my first instinctive thought will be to go where the Father waits for me, and where prayer can never go unblessed. Let me know that He knows my need before I ask. This will allow me, in great faith, to trust that He will give what His child requires. May the place of secret prayer become the most beloved spot on earth to me.

Lord! Hear me as I pray that You would bless the prayer closets of your believing people everywhere. Let Your wonderful revelation of the Father's tenderness free all Christians from the thought that prayer is a burden, and lead them to regard it as the highest privilege of their lives— a joy and a blessing. Bring back everyone who is discouraged because they cannot find You in prayer. Make them understand that all they have to do is to go to You with their emptiness, because You have everything to give, and You delight in doing it. Let their one thought be not what they have to take to the Father, but what the Father waits to give them.

Especially bless the inner chamber of all Your servants who are working for You as the place where God's truth and God's grace is revealed to them. Let them be anointed there with fresh oil daily. Let it be there that their strength is renewed and they receive in faith the blessings with which they are to bless their others. Lord, draw us all closer to You and the Father in prayer. Amen.

NOTES ON LESSON TWO

[1] Matthew 6:6
[2] Matthew 5:1-7:29
[3] Matthew 6:8
[4] Revelation 22:5
[5] Hebrews 11:27
[6] 1 John 5:15
[7] Philippians 4:17

PERSONAL NOTES

_____

_____

_____

LESSON 3

THE MODEL PRAYER

This, then, is how you should pray: 'Our
Father in heaven, hallowed be your
name,
your kingdom come, your will be done on
earth as it is in heaven.
Give us today our daily bread.
Forgive us our debts, as we also have
forgiven our debtors.
And lead us not into temptation, but
deliver us from the evil one'" [1]

Every teacher knows the power of example. A good
teacher not only tells the child what to do and how to
do it, but *shows* how it really can be done. Realizing
our weakness, our heavenly teacher has given us the
very words we are to take with us as we draw near to
our Father. We have in them a form of prayer that
contains the freshness and fullness of the eternal life.
It is so simple that a child can say it, and so divinely

rich that it encompasses all that God can give. A model and inspiration for all other prayer, it draws us at the same time back to itself as the deepest utterance of our souls before our God.

OUR FATHER IN HEAVEN

"Our Father in Heaven." To appreciate these words of adoration correctly, remember that none of the Old Testament saints in the Scriptures ever ventured to address God as Father. These words place us at once in the center of the wonderful revelation that Jesus came to make: *His Father is our Father, too.* They are the essence of redemption—Christ delivers us from the curse[2] so that we can become the children of God. They explain the miracle of regeneration—the Spirit in the new birth gives us new life. They reveal the mystery of faith—before the redemption is accomplished or understood, the disciples speak the words that prepare them for the blessed experience yet to come.

The opening words of this prayer are the key to the whole prayer and to all prayer. It takes time and life to study them; it will take eternity to understand them fully.

The knowledge of God's Father-love is the first and simplest, but also the last and highest lesson in the school of prayer. Prayer begins in a personal relationship with the living God as well as a personal, conscious, fellowship of love with Him. In the knowledge of God's fatherliness revealed by the Holy Spirit, the power of prayer will root and grow. The life of prayer has its joy in the infinite tenderness, care, and patience of an infinite Father who is ready to hear and to help.

18

Our Father in heaven. Wait until the Spirit has made these words spirit and truth to you, filling your heart and life. Then you will indeed be within the veil, in the secret place of power where prayer always prevails.

HALLOWED BE YOUR NAME

There is something about the sound of "hallowed be Your name" that strikes us at once. While we ordinarily bring our own needs to God in prayer before thinking of what belongs to God and His interests, the Master reverses the order. First *Your* name, *Your* kingdom, *Your* will; then give *us*, lead *us*, deliver *us*. The lesson is of more importance than we think. In true worship the Father must be first and He must be everything. The sooner we learn to forget ourselves so that He may be glorified, the richer our own blessing in prayer will be. No one ever loses anything by sacrificing for the Father. This must influence all our prayer.

There are two sorts of prayer: personal and intercessory. The latter ordinarily occupies the lesser part of our time and energy. This should not be. Christ has opened the school of prayer especially to train intercessors for the great work of bringing down, by their faith and prayer, the blessings of His work and love to the world. There can be no deep growth in prayer unless this is our aim.

A child may ask its father to provide only what it needs for itself. But this child soon learns to ask for the needs of its brother or sister, too. The grown-up son or daughter who lives only for the father's interests and takes charge of the father's business asks more largely and gets everything they ask. Jesus wants to train us for the blessed life of consecration and service in which all our interests are subordinate to the name, the kingdom, and the will of the Father. Live for this. Let each "Our Father." be followed in the same breath by "*Your* name, *Your* kingdom, *Your* Will."

THE HALLOWED NAME

What name is hallowed? This new name of *Father*. The word *holy* is the central word of the Old Testament. *Father is* the central word of the New Testament. In this name of love, all the holiness and glory of God are revealed.

How is the name to be hallowed? By God himself: "I will *hallow* my great name which you have profaned" [see Endnote[3]]. Our prayer must be for God to reveal the holiness, the divine power, and the hidden glory of His name in us, in all His children, and in the world. The Spirit of the Father is the *Holy* Spirit. It is only when we yield ourselves to be led by *Him*, that the Father's name will be *hallowed* in our prayers and our lives. Let us learn this prayer: "Our Father, hallowed be Your name."

YOUR KINGDOM COME

The Father is a king who has a kingdom. The children and heirs of a king have no higher ambition than the glory of their father's kingdom. In time of war or danger, this becomes their passion, they can think of nothing else. The children of the Father are here in the enemy's territory, where the kingdom that is in heaven has not yet been fully manifested. What is more natural than when they learn to hallow the Father's name they cry with deep enthusiasm, "Your kingdom come."

The coming of the kingdom is the one great event on which the revelation of the Father's glory, the blessedness of His children, and the salvation of the world depend. The coming of the kingdom also depends on our prayers. Let us join in the deep, longing, cry of the redeemed, "Your kingdom come," that we have learned in the school of Christ.

YOUR WILL BE DONE ON EARTH AS IT IS IN HEAVEN

The petition that God's will be done on earth as in heaven is too frequently applied alone to the *suffering* of God's will [see Endnote⁴]. In heaven God's will *is done,* and the Master teaches the child to ask that God's will may be done on earth just as it is in heaven—that is, in the spirit of adoring submission and ready obedience.

Because the will of God is the glory of heaven, doing His will brings the blessedness of heaven. As the will is done, the kingdom of heaven comes into the heart. Wherever faith has accepted the Father's love, obedience accepts the Father's will. The surrender to, and the prayer for, a life of heaven-like obedience is the spirit of childlike prayer.

Give Us Today Our Daily Bread

When we have yielded ourselves to the Father in concern for His name, His kingdom, and His will, we have full liberty to ask for our daily bread. A master cares for the food of his servant, as does a general for his soldiers, or a father for his child. The Father in heaven will care for the children who have given themselves up in prayer to His interests. We may in full confidence say, "Father, I live for your honor and your work. I know you care for me."

Consecration to God and His will gives wonderful liberty in prayer for temporal things. The whole earthly life is given over to the Father's loving care.

Forgive Us Our Debts, As We Also Have Forgiven Our Debtors

As food is the first need of the body, so forgiveness is for the soul. God's provision for the one is as sure as for the other. We are children, but we are sinners, too. We owe our right of access to the Father's presence to the precious blood of Jesus and the forgiveness it has won for us.

Beware of the prayer for forgiveness becoming a formality. Only that which is sincerely confessed is really forgiven. Let us in faith accept the forgiveness as promised. It is a spiritual reality, an actual transaction between God and us, giving us entrance into all the Father's love with all the privileges of His children. Such forgiveness is impossible without a forgiving spirit toward others. In each prayer to the Father, we must be able to say that we know of no one whom we do not heartily love.

LEAD US NOT INTO TEMPTATION, BUT DELIVER US FROM THE EVIL ONE

All our personal needs are supplied through the provision of our daily bread, the pardon of our sins, and the protection from all temptation and the power of the evil one. The prayer for bread and pardon must be accompanied by surrendering to live in holy obedience to the Father's will in all things. A prayer of belief that everything will be kept by the power of the indwelling Spirit from the power of the evil one should also be offered.

PRAY LIKE THIS TO YOUR FATHER

Jesus wants you to pray like this to your Father in heaven. O let His name, kingdom, and will have the first place in your love. In response, God will *provide* for you, *pardon* you, and *love* you. So the prayer will lead you to the true child-life—the Father giving everything *to* the child and being everything *for* the child.

You will then understand how Father and child— the *Your* and the *my*—are one. The heart that begins its prayer with the God-devoted *Your,* will have the power to speak out in faith the *my*, too.

Such prayer will indeed be the fellowship and interchange of love, always bringing you back in trust and worship to Him who is not only the beginning but the end.[5] *"For Yours is the kingdom and the power and the glory forever. Amen."*

LORD, TEACH US TO PRAY

O Jesus! The only begotten Son. Teach us to pray, "Our Father." We thank You for these living, blessed, words that You have given us. We thank You for everyone who through these words has learned to know and worship the Father, and for what these people have meant to us, Lord. We feel as if we need years in Your school to learn each separate lesson, because Your lessons are so profound. But, instead, we look to You to lead us more deeply into their meaning. Please do this, Lord. We ask it for Your name's sake—Your name is Son of the Father.

Lord! Once you said, "No one knows the Son except the Father, and no one knows the Father except the Son and those to whom the Son chooses to reveal Him."⁶ You also said, "I made Your name known to them, and I will make it known, so that the love with which You have loved Me may be in them, and I in them."⁷

Lord Jesus! Reveal the Father to us. Let His name and His infinite Father-love—the love with which He loved You—be in us. Then we will be able to rightly say, "Our Father." Then we will understand Your teaching and the first spontaneous breathing of our hearts will be, "Our Father, Your name, Your kingdom and Your will." And then we will bring our needs, our sins, and our temptations to Him in the confidence that the love of such a Father cares for each of us.

Blessed Lord! We are Your students, and we trust You. Please teach us to pray, Our Father. Amen.

NOTES ON LESSON THREE

[1] Matthew 6:9-13

[2] Galatians 3:13

3 Ezekiel 36:23 — Most Bible versions read: "I will sanctify My great name, . . . which you have profaned . . ." The NIV reads: "I will show the holiness of my great name, . . ." Sanctify means to set apart for sacred use, or to make holy. Hallow means to make or set apart as holy. So the words are somewhat interchangeable, although there is a slight difference in their meanings.

4 Probably refers to submissively surrendering to God's will, allowing Him to do what He wills regardless of your own will. Slight possibility that it refers to the suffering that is sometimes involved in obeying the will of God. In Acts 9:16 it is recorded that Jesus said to Ananias about the converted Saul, "I will show him how much he must suffer for my name."

[5] Revelation 21:6

[6] Matthew 11:27

[7] John 17:26, NRSV

PERSONAL NOTES

_____

_____

_____

Lesson 4

The Certain Answer to Prayer

*"Ask and it will be given to you; seek and
you will find; knock and the door will be
opened to you. For everyone who asks
receives; he who seeks finds; and to him
who knocks, the door will be opened."[1]
When you ask, you do not receive,
because you ask with wrong motives.[2]*

Our Lord returns here in the Sermon on the Mount
to speak of prayer a second time. The first time He
spoke of the Father who is found in secret and who
rewards openly. Jesus also gave us the pattern of
prayer.[3] Here He wants to teach us what in all the
Scriptures is considered the chief thing in prayer—the
assurance that prayer will be heard and answered.

Observe how He uses words that mean almost the
same thing and repeats the promise each time so
distinctly: "it *will* be given to you, you *will* find, it *will*

be opened to you." He then gives a law of the kingdom as grounds for such assurance: "For everyone who asks *receives;* he who seeks *finds*; to him who knocks, the door *will be opened.* " We cannot help but feel that in this sixfold repetition He wants to impress this one truth deeply on our minds—*We may and must most confidently expect an answer to our prayer.*

Everyone that asks, receives. Next to the revelation of the Father's love, there is not a more important lesson than this in the whole course of the school of prayer.

ASK, SEEK, KNOCK

A difference in meaning has been sought by some in the three words the Lord uses: *ask, seek, knock.* If it was indeed His purpose for these three words to have three distinct meanings, then the first, *ask,* refers to the gifts we pray for. But we may ask and receive the gift without the giver. *Seek* is the word the Scriptures often use of God Himself.[4] Christ assures us that we can find Him. But it is not enough to find God in time of need without coming into abiding fellowship with Him. *Knock* refers to admission to dwell with Him and in Him. Asking and receiving the gift would thus lead to seeking and finding the giver, and from there to the knocking on and opening of the door to the Father's home and love.

One thing is certain, the Lord wants us to believe most surely that asking, seeking, and knocking cannot be in vain. Receiving an answer, finding God, and the opening of His heart and home are the certain fruits of prayer.

That the Lord should have thought it necessary to repeat the truth in so many forms is a lesson of deep importance. It proves that He knows our hearts. He knows that doubt and distrust toward Him are natural to us and that we view prayer as religious work without expecting an answer. He also knows that we believe prayer is something spiritually too difficult for halfhearted disciples, even though they believe that God hears prayer and answers it.

At the very beginning of His instruction, therefore, Jesus endeavors to lodge this truth deeply into the hearts of those who want to learn to pray—*prayer accomplishes a great deal.* Ask and you will receive—*everyone* who asks, receives. This is the eternal law of the kingdom. If you ask and receive not, it must be because there is something wrong or missing in the prayer. Let the Word and the Spirit teach you to pray properly. But do not lose the confidence He wants to give you, that everyone who asks, receives.

ASK AND IT WILL BE GIVEN TO YOU

In Christ's school, there is no mightier encouragement of persevering in prayer than to be told that if we ask, what we ask for will be given to us. As a child has to prove a sum to be correct, so the proof that we have prayed correctly is *our answer.* If we ask and get no answer, it is because we have not learned to pray properly. Let every learner in the school of Christ, therefore, take the Master's Word in all simplicity: Everyone who asks, receives.

Christ had good reasons for speaking so unconditionally. Be careful not to weaken the Word with human wisdom. When He tells us heavenly things, believe Him. His Word will explain itself to the one who believes it fully. If questions and difficulties arise, don't try to settle them before accepting the Word. Let us entrust them all to Him. He will solve them. Our work is to accept and believe His promise completely. Let our inner chamber be inscribed with that promise in letters of light.

Two Parts to Prayer

According to the teaching of the Master, prayer consists of two parts: a human side and a divine side. The human side is the asking, the divine is the giving. Or, to look at both from the human side, there is the asking and the receiving—the two halves that make up a whole. It is as if He wants to tell us that we are not to rest without an answer, because it is the will of God and the rule in the Father's family that every childlike, believing, petition is granted.

If no answer comes, we are not to sit down in resignation and suppose that it is not God's will to give us an answer. There must be something in the prayer that is not as God would have it. We must seek for guidance to pray so that the answer will come. It is far easier for the flesh to submit without the answer, than to yield itself to being searched and purified by the Spirit until it has learned to pray the prayer of faith.

One of the terrible marks of the diseased state of Christian life these days is that there are so many who are content without the distinct experience of answer to prayer. They pray daily, they ask many things, and they trust that some of them will be heard. But they know little of direct, definite, answer to prayer as the rule of daily life.

The Father seeks daily communion with His children so that He can listen to and grant their petitions. He wills that we come to Him day by day with distinct requests. He wills day by day to do what I ask. It was in His answer to prayer that the saints learned to know God as the living one, and were stirred to praise and love Him.[5] Our Teacher waits to imprint this on our minds: Prayer and its answer—the child asking and the Father giving—belong to each other.

ALWAYS AN ANSWER

There may be cases in which the answer is a refusal because the request is not according to God's Word, such as when Moses asked to enter Canaan. *But there was still an answer.* God did not leave His servant in uncertainty as to His will. The gods of the heathen are dumb and cannot speak. Our Father lets His children know when He cannot give them what they ask. They then withdraw their petition as the Son did in Gethsemane.

Both Moses the servant and Christ the Son knew that what they asked was not according to what the Lord had spoken. Their prayer was the humble request that the decision be changed. By His Word and Spirit, God will teach those who are teachable, and who give Him time, whether their request is according to His will or not. Withdraw the request if it is not according to God's will, or persevere until the answer comes. *Prayer is supposed to have an answer.* It is in prayer and its answer that the interchange of love between the Father and His child takes place.

31

DIFFICULT TO GRASP THE PROMISES

How deeply our hearts must be estranged from God that we should find it so difficult to grasp such promises.. Even though we accept the words and believe their truth, the faith of the heart that fully possesses them and rejoices in them comes so slowly. It is because our spiritual life is still so weak and our capacity for accepting God's thoughts is so feeble. Let us look to Christ to teach us as none but He can teach.

Simply take His words and trust Him by His Spirit to make them life and power within us. They will enter our inner being and allow the spiritual divine reality of the truth they contain to take possession of us. We should not be content until every petition we offer is carried to heaven on Jesus' own words: "Ask and it will be given to you."

LEARN THE LESSON OF ANSWERED PRAYER

Learn this lesson well. Take Jesus' words just as they were spoken. Do not let human reason weaken their force. Take them and believe them just as Jesus gave them. In due time, He will teach you how to understand them fully. For now you should begin by implicitly believing them.

Take time in prayer to listen to His voice. Don't let the feeble experiences of unbelief limit what faith can expect.

Seek not only in prayer, but at all times, to accept joyfully the assurance that your prayer on earth and God's answer in heaven are meant for each other. Trust Christ to teach you to pray so that the answer can come. He will do it if you hold fast to the word He gives us: "Everyone who asks receives."

LORD, TEACH US TO PRAY

O Lord Jesus! Teach me to understand and believe what You have promised me. You know the reasons that churn in my heart when I don't receive an answer to my prayer. When that happens, I too often believe that my prayer is not in harmony with the Father's will, that perhaps You want to give me something better, or that prayer as fellowship with God should be enough blessing to me without an answer. And yet, my blessed Lord, I find in Your teaching that You said plainly that prayer may and must *expect an answer. You assure us that this is the fellowship of a child with the Father*—The child asks and the Father gives.

Blessed Lord! Your words are faithful and true. It must be because I am not praying correctly that my experience of answered prayer is small. It must be because I live too little in the Spirit that my prayer is too little in the Spirit, and my power for the prayer of faith is lacking.

Lord! Teach me to pray. Lord Jesus, I trust You to teach me to pray in faith.

Lord! Teach me this lesson—Everyone who asks, receives. *Amen.*

NOTES ON LESSON FOUR

[1] Matthew 7:7-8

[2] James 4:3

[3] Matthew 6:5-15

[4] 2 Chronicles 15:12, Psalm 9:10, Proverbs 28:5, Isaiah 55:6, Jeremiah 29:13, Romans 10:20, Hebrews 11:6

[5] Psalm 34, 66:19, 116:1

PERSONAL NOTES

_____

_____

_____

_____

_____

_____

_____

_____

LESSON 5

THE
INFINITE FATHERLINESS OF GOD

*"Which of you, if his son asks for bread,
will give him a stone? Or if he asks for a
fish, will give him a snake? If you, then,
though you are evil, know how to give
good gifts to your children, how much
more will your Father in heaven give
good gifts to those who ask him!"[1]*

In these words our Lord proceeds further to confirm
what He had said about the certainty of an answer to
prayer. To remove all doubt and to show us on what
sure ground His promise rests, He appeals to what
everyone has seen and experienced here on earth.
Because we are all children we know what we expected
of our parents. Because we are parents or continually
see them in action, we consider it the most natural thing
in the world for parents to listen to their child. The
Lord asks us to look up from earthly parents—of whom

even the best are sinners—and calculate *how much more* the heavenly Father will give good gifts to those who ask Him.

Jesus wants us to see that because God is greater than sinful humanity, our assurance that He will more surely than any earthly parent grant our childlike petitions should be greater. As much greater as God is than us, so *much surer* is it that prayer will be heard by the Father in heaven than a request will be by a father or mother on earth.

A SIMPLE BUT DEEP PARABLE

Although this parable is simple and intelligible, it contains a deep and spiritual teaching. The request of a child owes its influence entirely to the relation in which it stands to the parent. The request can exert that influence only when the child is really living in that relationship and in the home, in the love, and in the service of the parents.

The power of the promise, "Ask and it will be given to you," lies in the loving relationship between us as children and our Father in heaven. When we live and walk in that relationship, the prayer of faith and its answer will be the natural result. So this lesson in the school of prayer is this—*Live as a child of God and you will be able to pray and most assuredly be heard as a child.*

WHAT IS THE TRUE CHILD-LIFE?

The answer to the question "What is the true child-life?" can be found in any home. Children who forsake their parent's home, finding no pleasure in the presence and love of their parents or in obeying them, and who still expect to get whatever they asks for, will surely be disappointed. Conversely, children who find the joy of their life in the conversation, will, honor, and love of their parents will find that it is their parents' joy to grant their requests.

The Scripture says, "all who are led by the Spirit of God are children of God."[2] The childlike privilege of asking for everything is inseparable from the childlike life under the leading of the Spirit. Those who give themselves to be led by the Spirit in their lives will be led by Him in their prayers, too. They will then find that Father-like giving is the divine response to childlike living.

CHILDLIKE LIVING

To see what this childlike living is, in which childlike asking and believing have their grounds, we should listen to what our Lord teaches in the Sermon on the Mount about the Father and His children. In the Sermon, the prayer-promises are imbedded in the life-precepts. The two are inseparable, they form one whole.

The only person who can count on the fulfillment of the promise is the person who accepts all that the Lord has connected with it. It is as if in speaking the word, "Ask and you will receive," He says, in effect, "I give these promises to those whom I have pictured in their childlike poverty and purity, and of whom I have said, 'They shall be called the children of God'"(see the Beatitudes[3]).

CONFORMING TO CHILDLIKE LIVING

Someone may ask, "If it is necessary for us to conform to childlike living, won't many give up all hope of answers to prayer?" The difficulty is removed if we think again of the blessed relationship of parent and child. Although there is a great difference among children because age or talent, a child basically is weak. Because of that, the Lord does not demand that we fulfill the law perfectly. All He requires is our childlike and wholehearted surrender to live as children with Him in obedience and truth. He asks nothing more, but will accept nothing less.

The Father must have the child's whole heart. When this is given and He sees us with honest purpose and steady will, seeking to be and live as children in everything, then our prayer will count with Him as the prayer of a child. If we simply and honestly begin to study the Sermon on the Mount and take it as our guide in life, we will find, notwithstanding weakness and failure, an ever growing liberty to claim the fulfillment of its promises in regard to prayer. In the names of the Father and the Son, we have the pledge that our petitions will be granted.

This is the one chief thought on which Jesus dwells here, and which He would like all of His students to consider. He wants us to see that the secret of effective prayer is to have the heart filled with the Father-love of God. It is not enough for us to know that God is a Father. It is necessary for us to take time to meditate on what that name implies.

To do so, we must take the best earthly parents we know, contemplating carefully the tenderness and love with which they regard the request of their child and the love and joy with which they grant every reasonable desire. Then, as we think in adoring worship of the infinite love and fatherliness of God, we must consider with *how much more* tenderness and joy *He* regards our requests and gives us what we ask for.

GOD'S DIVINE ATTITUDE BEYOND OUR COMPREHENSION

The Lord wants us to see how much this divine attitude is beyond our comprehension and to feel how impossible it is for us to understand God's readiness to hear us. Then He wants us to come and open our hearts for the Holy Spirit to fill them with God's Father-love. Let us do this not only when we want to pray, but let us yield heart and life to dwell in that love.

Those who only want to know the love of the Father when they have something to ask will be disappointed. But whoever lets God always be the Father in everything, living their whole life in the Father's presence and love, will discover that such a life in God's infinite fatherliness and continual answers to prayer are inseparable.

WE KNOW LITTLE ABOUT DAILY ANSWERS TO PRAYERS

We are beginning to see why we know so little about daily answers to prayer. The chief lesson the Lord has for you in His school centers on the name of Father. You must learn to say, "Abba, Father."[4] and "Our [My] Father who is in heaven." Whoever can say this has the key to all prayer.

The Father listens in all the compassion with which parents listen to a weak or sickly child, in all the joy with which they hear a stammering child, in all the gentle patience with which they tolerate a thoughtless child. You must meditate upon the heart of your Father until your every prayer goes upward on the faith of this divine word: "how much more will your Father in heaven give good gifts to those who ask him."[5]

LORD, TEACH US TO PRAY

Blessed Lord! Though this is one of the first and simplest lessons in Your school, it is one of the hardest for our hearts to learn. We know so little of the love of the Father.

Lord! Teach us to live in such a way that the Father and His love may be nearer, clearer, and dearer to us than the love of any earthly parent. Let Your assurance of His hearing our prayers give us much more confidence in Him than in any earthly parent, because He is infinitely greater than any human being.

Lord! Show us that it is only our unchildlike distance from the Father that hinders the answer to prayer and leads us on to the true life of God's children.

Lord Jesus! It is father-like love that awakens childlike trust. Reveal the Father and His tender love to us, so that we may become childlike and experience how in the child's life lies the power of prayer.

Blessed Son of God! The Father loves You and has given You all authority in heaven and on earth.[6] And because You love the Father and have

*done all the things He commanded You to do, You
have the power to ask for anything.*

*Lord! Give us Your Spirit, the Spirit of the Son.
Make us as childlike as You were on earth. Let
our prayers be breathed in the faith that—just as
heaven is higher than earth—God's Father-love
and His readiness to give us what we ask for
surpass anything we can imagine. Amen.*

[AUTHOR'S NOTE]

OUR FATHER IN HEAVEN

"Our Father who is in heaven." Alas, we speak it
only as a reverential homage. We think of it as a figure
borrowed from an earthly life, and only in some faint
and shallow meaning to be used of God. We are afraid
to take God as our tender Father. We think of Him as a
schoolmaster or an inspector, who knows nothing about
us except through our lessons.

OPEN THE EARS OF YOUR HEART

Open the ears of your heart, timid child of God.
You are not supposed to learn to be holy as a hard lesson
at school so you can make God think well of you. You
are to learn it at home with the Father to help you. God
loves you not because you are clever or good, but
because He is *your Father.*

The Cross of Christ does not *make* God love you.
It is the *outcome* of His love to you. He loves all His
children—the clumsiest, the dullest, and the worst. His
love lies underneath everything. You must grasp it as
the solid foundation of your religious life, not growing

41

up *into* that love, but growing up *out of it*. You must begin there or your beginning will come to nothing.

Grasp this mightily. You must go beyond yourself for any hope, strength, or confidence. And what hope, what strength, what confidence may be yours when you begin with *Our Father who is in heaven*. You need to feel the tenderness and helpfulness that lie in these words.

OUR FATHER

Meditate on the words *our Father*. Say them over to yourself until you feel something of their wonderful truth. They mean that you are bound to God by the closest and tenderest relationship, and that you have a right to His love, His power, and His blessings in a way no one else could give you. Imagine the boldness with which you can approach Him. Imagine the great things you have a right to ask for.

The words "our Father" mean that all His infinite love, patience, and wisdom reach down to help *you*. There is infinitely more implied by this relationship then the possibility of holiness.

YOUR FATHER'S PATIENT LOVE

Begin in the patient love of your Father. Think about how He knows you personally, as an individual with all your peculiarities, your weaknesses, and your difficulties. Earthly masters judge by the result, but your Father judges by the effort. Failure does not always mean fault. He knows how much things cost you and weighs them carefully where others would not.

Think about how His great love understands the poor beginnings of His little ones, clumsy and simple as they may seem to others. All this and infinitely more lies in this blessed relationship. Do not be afraid to claim it all as your own.

NOTES ON LESSON FIVE

[1] Matthew 7:9-11
[2] Romans 8:14, NRSV
[3] Matthew 5:3-11
[4] Romans 8:15, Galatians 4:6
[5] Matthew 7:11
[6] Matthew 28:18

PERSONAL NOTES

_____

_____

_____

_____

_____

_____

LESSON 6

THE ALL-COMPREHENSIVE GIFT

*"If you then, though you are evil, know
how to give good gifts to your children,
how much more will your Father in
heaven give the Holy Spirit to those who
ask him!"*[1]

In the Sermon on the Mount, the Lord had already given utterance to his wonderful "How much more?"[2] Here in Luke, where He repeats the question, there is a difference. Instead of speaking as He did then of giving *good gifts,* He says, "How much more will your Father in heaven give *the Holy Spirit?"* He thus teaches us that the chief and the best of these gifts is the Holy Spirit, or rather, that in this gift all others are contained.

The Holy Spirit is the first of the Father's gifts and the one He delights most in giving. The Holy Spirit is therefore the gift we should seek first.

THE PROMISE OF THE FATHER

We can easily understand the unspeakable worth of this gift. Jesus spoke of the Spirit as *"the promise of My Father,"*[3] the one promise in which God's fatherhood revealed itself. The best gift a good and wise earthly father can bestow on a child is his own spirit—similarly with a mother and daughter. This is the great object of a good father—to reproduce in his son something of his own disposition and character. If the son is to know and understand his father, if he is to enter into his will and plans, if he is to have his highest joy in the father and the father in him, he must be of one mind and spirit with him.

It is impossible to conceive of God bestowing any higher gift on His child than His own Spirit. God is what He is through His Spirit—the Spirit is the very life of God. Just think what it means for God to give His own Spirit to His child on earth.

THE GLORY OF JESUS WAS THE SPIRIT OF THE FATHER

The glory of Jesus as a Son on earth was that the Spirit of the Father was in Him. At His baptism in the Jordan, the voice proclaiming Him the beloved Son and the Spirit descending upon Him were united. And so the apostle Paul says of us, "because you are children, God has sent the Spirit of his Son into our hearts, crying, "Abba. Father."[4]

A king and queen seek in the whole education of their children to call forth a royal spirit in them. Our Father in heaven desires to educate us as His children

46

for the holy, heavenly, life in which He dwells. For this purpose He gives us His own Spirit from the depths of His heart.

Spirit of the Father and the Son

Jesus' whole purpose after He made atonement with His own blood was to enter into God's presence and obtain the Holy Spirit for us, sending Him down to dwell in us. Because He is the Spirit of the Father and the Son, the whole life and love of the Father and Son are in Him. Coming down among us, He lifts us up into their fellowship.

As the Spirit of the Father, He fills our hearts with the love with which the Father loved the Son, and teaches us to live in it. As the Spirit of the Son, He breathes into us the childlike liberty, devotion, and obedience in which the Son lived on earth. The Father can bestow no higher or more wonderful gift than this— His own Holy Spirit, the Spirit of Sonship.[5]

First and Chief Gift of the Father

This truth naturally suggests that this first and chief gift of God must be the first and chief object of all prayer. The one necessary element in the spiritual life is the Holy Spirit. All the fullness is in Jesus. His is the fullness of grace and truth from which we receive grace for grace. The Holy Spirit is the appointed intermediary whose special work is to convey Christ and everything there is in Him to us. He is the Spirit of life in Christ Jesus.[6]

If we yield ourselves entirely to the will of the Spirit and let Him have His way with us, He will manifest the life of Christ within us.[7] He will do this with a divine power, maintaining the life of Christ in us in uninterrupted continuity. If there is one thing we should pray for that will draw us to the Father's throne and keep us there, it is the Holy Spirit.

MEETS THE BELIEVER'S NEEDS

The Spirit meets the believer's every need in the variety of gifts that He has to dispense. Just think of the names He bears. He is the Spirit of:

- *Grace,*[8] who reveals and imparts all of the grace there is in Jesus
- *Faith,*[9] who teaches us to begin, go on, and increase in believing
- *Adoption*[10] *and assurance,*[11] who witnesses that we are God's children, and inspires our confiding in Him and our confident "Abba, Father."
- *Truth,*[12] who leads us to accept each word of God in truth
- *Prayer,*[13] through whom we speak with the Father so that we may be heard
- *Judgment,*[14] who searches out hearts and convicts us of sin
- *Holiness,*[15] who manifests and communicates the Father's holy presence within us
- *Power,*[16] who makes us testify boldly and work effectively in the Father's service
- *Glory,*[17] who is the pledge of our inheritance and prepares us for the glory to come

Surely the child of God needs only one thing to be able to really live as a child of God—to be filled with this Holy Spirit.

The Lesson Jesus Teaches in His School

The lesson that Jesus teaches in His school is that the Father is longing to give the Holy Spirit to us if we will simply ask in childlike dependence on what He says: "If you . . . know how to give good gifts to your children, how much more will your Father in heaven give the Holy Spirit to those who ask him!" In the words of God's promise, "I will pour out my Spirit *abundantly*,"[18] and in His command, "Be *filled* with the Spirit,"[19] we know what God is ready to give us.

As God's children, we have already received the Spirit. But we still need to pray for His special gifts as we require them. We need to pray also for His complete possession and unceasing guidance.[20] We are like a branch that is already filled with the sap of the vine and is crying for the continued and increasing flow of that sap. Just as the branch needs more sap to bring its fruit to perfection, the believer, rejoicing in the possession of the Spirit, still thirsts and cries for more.

What our great teacher would like us to learn in this situation is that we should expect nothing less than God's promise and God's command in answer to our prayer. We must be filled abundantly. Christ wants us to ask this in the assurance that the wonderful *"how much more"* of God's Father-love is a pledge that when we ask we will most certainly receive.

PRAYING TO BE FILLED WITH THE SPIRIT

As we pray to be filled with the Spirit, we shouldn't look for the answer in our feelings. All spiritual blessings must be received—that is, accepted or taken—in faith [see Endnote[21]].

Believe that the Father *gives* the Holy Spirit to His praying child. Even while I pray, I must say in faith, "I have what I ask, and the fullness of the Spirit is mine."[22] Let us continue unshakably in this faith. On the strength of God's Word we know that we have what we ask.[23]

We should be thankful that we have been heard and thankful for what we have received and now possess. Continue praying in belief that the blessing that has already been given to us will break through and fill our entire being. It is in such believing thanksgiving and prayer[24] that our souls open up and the Spirit takes entire and undisturbed possession of them. Such prayer not only asks and hopes for, but also takes, holds, and inherits the full blessing. In all our prayer let us remember the lesson the Savior teaches us—*the Father wants us to be filled with His Spirit, and He delights in giving Him to us.*

PRAYING FOR OUTPOURING OF THE HOLY SPIRIT

Once we have learned to believe this for ourselves, we can take the liberty and power from the treasure held for us in heaven to pray for the outpouring of the Spirit on the Church, on all flesh, on individuals, or on special efforts.[25] Once we have learned to know the Father in prayer for ourselves, we learn to pray most confidently for others, too. The Father gives the Holy Spirit most to those who ask that He be given to others.

LORD, TEACH US TO PRAY

Father in heaven! You sent Your Son to reveal Yourself to us—your Father-love and everything that love has for us. Christ taught us that the gift above all gifts that You want to give us in answer to prayer is the Holy Spirit.

O my Father! There is nothing I desire so much as to be filled with the Holy Spirit. The blessings He brings are so unspeakable. They are just what I need. He fills the heart with You and with Your love. I long for this. He breathes the mind and life of Christ into me, so that I can live as He did, in and for Your love. I long for this. He supplies power from heaven for all my walk and work. I long for this. O Father! Please give me the fullness of Your Spirit today.

Father! I base this request on the words of my Lord, "How much more will Your Father in heaven give the Holy Spirit."[26] I believe that You hear my prayer, and that I receive now just what I am asking for.

Father! I receive it by faith in You and Your Word. The fullness of your Spirit is mine.

I receive this gift today as a faith gift. In faith, I believe You work everything You have promised through the Spirit, and that You delight in breathing Your Spirit into Your waiting children as we fellowship with You. Amen.

NOTES ON LESSON SIX

[1] Luke 11:13
[2] Matthew 7:11
[3] Luke 24:49, Acts 1:4
[4] Galatians 4:6
[5] Romans 8:15, NIV
[6] Romans 8:2
[7] Colossians 1:27
[8] Hebrews 10:29
[9] 2 Corinthians 4:13
[10] Romans 8:15

[11] Expression "Spirit of assurance" not found. Probably taken from 1 Thessalonians 1:5, which reads in part: "For our gospel did not come to you in word only, but also in power, and in the Holy Spirit and in much assurance."

[12] John 14:17, 15:26, 16:13; 1 John 4:6

[13] Expression "Spirit of prayer" not found. Probably taken from Romans 8:26 or Ephesians 6:18, which reads: "Praying always with all prayer and supplication in the Spirit." Might also be from Ephesians 2:2, which reads: "For through Him [Christ] we both have access to the Father by one Spirit."

[14] Expression "Spirit of judgment" found only in Isaiah 4:4 in KJV and NKJV, and in Isaiah 28:6 in KJV. See also John 16:8-11.

[15] Romans 1:4

[16] Expression "Spirit of power" not found. Probably taken from Luke 24:49 and Acts 1:8, which states: "you will receive power when the Holy Spirit comes on you; and you will be my witnesses in Jerusalem, and in all Judea and Samaria, and to the ends of the earth."

[17] 1 Peter 4:14

[18] Exact expression not found, probably from Titus 3:6, which states: "whom [Holy Spirit] He [God] poured out on us abundantly through Jesus Christ our Savior." See also Joel 2:28-29.

[19] Ephesians 5:18

[20] Romans 8:14, Galatians 5:18

[21] The Greek word for receiving and taking is the same. When Jesus said, "everyone who asks *receives*" (Matthew 7:8), He used the same verb as at the covenant meal, "*take* and eat" (Matthew 26:26), or on the resurrection morning, "*Receive* (accept, take) the Holy Spirit" (John 20:22). Receiving not only implies God's giving, but our acceptance.

[22] Mark 11:24

[23] 1 John 5:15

[24] Philippians 4:6

[25] Joel 2:28, Acts 2:17

[26] Luke 11:13

PERSONAL NOTES

_____

_____

_____

_____

_____

LESSON 7

THE BOLDNESS OF GOD'S FRIENDS

*Then he said to them, "Suppose one of
you has a friend, and he goes to him at
midnight and says, 'Friend, lend me three
loaves of bread,
because a friend of mine on a journey has
come to me, and I have nothing to set
before him.'*
*"Then the one inside answers, 'Don't
bother me. The door is already locked,
and my children are with me in bed. I
can't get up and give you anything.'*
*I tell you, though he will not get up and
give him the bread because he is his
friend, yet because of the man's boldness
he will get up and give him as much as he
needs.*[1]

The first teaching on prayer our Lord gave to His disciples was in the Sermon on the Mount.[2] It was nearly a year later that the disciples asked Jesus to teach them to pray.[3] In answer, He gave them the *Our Father*[4] [Lord's prayer] a second time to show them *what* to pray. He then spoke of *how* they should pray, and repeated what He formerly said of God's fatherliness and the certainty of an answer.

But in between He added the beautiful parable of the friend at midnight to teach them the twofold lesson that God does not only want us to pray for ourselves, but also for those who are perishing around us. In such intercession, great boldness of entreaty is often necessary and always lawful and pleasing to God. The parable is a perfect storehouse of instructions about true intercession. It contains:

- *The love* that seeks to help the needy around, us: "*A friend of mine* . . . has come to me"
- Then need that gives rise to the cry: "*I have nothing* to set before him"
- The confidence that help is available: "'"Suppose one of you has a *friend*, . . . and says, '*Friend*, lend me three loaves of bread'"
- *The unexpected refusal*: "I can't get up and give you anything."
- *The perseverance* that refuses to be refused: "because of his *persistence*"
- *The reward* of such prayer: "he will . . . give him *as much as he needs*"

Herein we find a perfect example of the prayer and faith in which God's blessing has so often been sought and found.

Let us confine ourselves to this chief thought—
Prayer is an appeal to the friendship of God. If we are
God's friends and go as friends to Him, we must prove
that we are friends of the needy. God's friendship to us
and ours to others go hand in hand. When we go to
God as this kind of friend, we may use the utmost liberty
in claiming an answer.

A TWOFOLD USE OF PRAYER

There is a twofold use of prayer. One is to obtain
strength and blessing for our own lives. The other is
the higher and true glory of prayer for which Christ
has taken us into His fellowship and teaching
intercession—*the royal power a child of God exercises
in heaven on behalf of others and even of the kingdom.*

We see in the Scriptures how it was in intercession
for others that Abraham, Moses, Samuel, Elijah, and
all the holy men and women of long ago proved that
they had power with God and prevailed. It is when we
give ourselves to be a blessing to others that we can
count on the blessing of God for ourselves. When we
go to God as a friend of the poor and the perishing, we
can count on His friendliness. The righteous person who
is a friend of the poor is a very special friend of God.
This gives wonderful liberty in prayer.

*"Lord! I have a needy friend whom I must help.
As a friend I have undertaken this help. In you I
have a friend whose kindness and riches I know
to be infinite. I am sure you will give me what I
ask. If I am ready to do for my friend whatever I
can even though I am a sinner, I know that you,
my heavenly friend, are ready to do so much more
to give me what I ask for."*

Pondering the friendship of God may not seem to reveal anything new about confident prayer after having studied the fatherhood of God. After all, a father is more than a friend. But if we consider it, pleading the friendship of God can open new wonders to us. It is so perfectly natural for children to obtain what they ask for from their father or mother that we almost call it the parent's duty to grant the children their requests.

With a friend, however, it is as if the kindness were freer, dependent on sympathy and character rather than on nature. In addition, the relationship of a child to its parents is one of perfect dependence. Two friends are more nearly on the same level. In teaching us the spiritual mystery of prayer, our Lord would rather have us approach God as those whom He has acknowledged as His friends and whose minds and lives are in sympathy with His.

FRIENDSHIP DEPENDS ON CONDUCT

We are still children even when we stray, but friendship depends on our conduct. "You are my friends if you do what I command."[5] "You see that his faith and his actions were working together, and his faith was made complete by what he did. And the scripture was fulfilled that says, "Abraham believed God, . . . and he was called God's friend.""[6] The Spirit, "*the same Spirit,*"[7] that leads us[8] also bears witness to our acceptance with God.[9]

That same Spirit helps us in prayer.[10] Life as a friend of God gives us the wonderful liberty to say, "I have a friend to whom I can go even at midnight." And how much better it is when I go in the very spirit of friendliness and kindness I look for in God, seeking to help my friend as I want God to help me.

58

GOD CHECKS OUR MOTIVE

When I go to God in prayer, He always looks at my motive for my petition. If it is merely for my own comfort or joy that I seek His grace, I may not receive it. But if I want Him to be glorified in my dispensing His blessings to others, I will not ask in vain. If I ask for others, but want to wait until God has made me so rich that it is no sacrifice or act of faith to aid them, I will not receive an answer. My prayer will be heard if I can say that I have already asked for help for a needy friend. Even though I don't have what I need, I have already begun the work of love, because I know I have a friend in heaven who will help me.

We do not understand how effective this plea is. When the friendship of earth looks in its need to the friendship of heaven, "He will . . . give him as much as he needs."[11]

WE DO NOT ALWAYS GET ALL AT ONCE WHAT WE ASK FOR

We do not, however, always get all at once what we ask for. The one way in which we can honor and enjoy our God is through *faith*. Intercession is part of faith's training school. There our friendship with people and with God is tested. It is seen whether our friendship with the needy is so real that we would sacrifice our rest and go even at midnight to obtain what they need.

Our friendship with God should be so clear that we can depend on Him not to turn us away, and so continue to pray until He answers.

Persevering Prayer

What a deep heavenly mystery persevering prayer is. The God who has promised and who longs to give the blessing holds it back. It is a matter of such deep importance to Him that His friends on earth should know and fully trust their rich friend in heaven.

Because of this, He trains them in the school of delayed answer to find out how their perseverance really does prevail. They can wield mighty power in heaven if they simply set themselves to it.

Faith That Does Not Receive the Promise

There is a faith that sees the promise and embraces it, but does not receive it.[12] When the answer to prayer does not come and the promise we most firmly trust appears to be fruitless, the trial of faith, more precious than gold, takes place.[13]

It is in this trial that the faith that has embraced the promise is purified, strengthened, and prepared in personal, holy, fellowship with the living God, to the end of giving Him glory. It takes and holds the promise until it has received the fulfillment in living truth of what it had requested from the unseen but living God.

Each child of God who is seeking to perform the work of love in their Father's service should take courage. The parent with the child, the teacher with the class, the Bible reader with the study circle, and the preacher with the congregation all bear the burden of hungry, perishing souls. Let them all take courage. That God should really require persevering prayer is at first very strange to us. But there is a real spiritual necessity for persevering.

LEARNING PERSEVERING PRAYER

To teach persevering prayer to us, the Master uses this almost strange parable. If the unfriendliness of a selfish earthly friend can be conquered by persistence, imagine how much more it will accomplish with our heavenly friend.

God loves to give us what we ask for, but is held back by our spiritual unfitness, our incapacity to possess what He has to give. Let us thank Him that in delaying His answer He is preparing us to assume our true position with Him and to exercise all our power. He is training us to live with Him in the fellowship of undoubting faith and trust, and to be truly the friends of God.

Let us securely hold the threefold cord that cannot be broken[14] —the hungry friend needing the help, the praying friend seeking the help, and the mighty friend in heaven loving to give us as much help as we need.

LORD, TEACH US TO PRAY

O my blessed Lord and Teacher! I must come to You in prayer—Your teaching is so glorious. But it is still too high for me to grasp. I must confess that my heart is too little to take in these thoughts of the wonderful boldness I may use with Your Father as my friend.

Lord Jesus! I trust You to give me Your Spirit with Your Word, and to make the Word quick and powerful in my heart. I desire to claim this promise from Your Word: "because of his persistence . . . he will give him as many as he needs."

Lord! Teach me to know the power of persevering prayer more. I know that in it, the Father allows for the time we need for the inner life to grow and ripen, so that His grace may be made for our very own. Through our persevering prayer, He trains us to exercise strong faith that does not let Him go even in the face of seeming disappointment. He wants to give us the wonderful liberty of knowing how truly He has made the dispensing of His gifts dependent on our prayers.

Lord! Teach me to not only know this in my mind, but to know it in spirit and truth.

Let it be the joy of my life to become the caretaker of my rich friend in heaven. Let me take care of all the hungry and perishing, even at midnight, because I know my friend always gives as much as is needed to those who persevere. Amen.

Notes on Lesson Seven

[1] Luke 11:5-8
[2] Matthew 6:9-13
[3] Luke 11:1
[4] Luke 11:1-4
[5] John 15:14
[6] James 2:22-23
[7] 1 Corinthians 12:4, 11
[8] Romans 8:14
[9] Romans 8:16
[10] Romans 8:26
[11] Luke 11:8
[12] Hebrews 11:13, 39
[13] 1 Peter 1:6-8
[14] Ecclesiastes 3:12

LESSON 8

PRAYER PROVIDES LABORERS

Then he said to his disciples, "The harvest
is plentiful but the workers are few.
Ask the Lord of the harvest, therefore, to
send out workers into his harvest field."[1]

The Lord frequently taught His disciples *that* they must pray and *how* they should pray. But He seldom told them *what* to pray. This He left to their sense of need and the leading of the Spirit. But in the above Scripture He expressly directs them to remember one thing. In view of the abundant harvest, and the need for reapers, they must ask the Lord of the harvest to send out laborers.

Just as in the parable of the friend at midnight, He wants them to understand that prayer is not to be selfish—it is the power through which blessing can come to others. The Father is Lord of the harvest. When we pray for the Holy Spirit, we must pray for Him to prepare and send laborers for the work.

IMPORTANT QUESTIONS ABOUT PRAYER

Why does He ask His disciples to pray for this? Could He not pray himself? Would not one prayer of His achieve more than a thousand of theirs? Is God, the Lord of the harvest, not aware of the need? Would He not, in His own good time, send laborers without the disciples' prayers?

Such important questions lead us into the deepest mysteries of prayer and its power in the kingdom of God. The answer to such questions will convince us that prayer is indeed a power on which the gathering of the harvest and the coming of the kingdom do in very truth depend.

EVERYTHING JESUS SPOKE WAS THE TRUTH

The Lord Jesus was Himself the truth—everything He spoke was the truth. It was "When He saw the crowds, He had compassion on them, because they were harassed and helpless, like sheep without a shepherd,"[2] that He called on the disciples to pray for laborers to be sent to them. He did so because He really believed that their prayer was needed and would help.

The veil that hides the invisible world from us was wonderfully transparent to the human holy soul of Jesus. He had looked long and deep and far into the hidden connection of cause and effect in the spiritual world. He had noted in God's Word how God called men like Abraham, Moses, Joshua, Samuel, and Daniel, giving them authority over people in His name. God also gave these men the authority to call the powers of heaven to their aid as they needed them.

Jesus knew that the work of God had been entrusted to these men of old and to Him for a time here upon earth. Now it was about to pass over into the hands of His disciples. He knew that when they were given responsibility for this work, it would not be a mere matter of form or show. The success of the work would actually depend on them and their faithfulness.

JESUS AS A SINGLE INDIVIDUAL

As a single individual, within the limitations of a human body and a human life, Jesus feels how little a short visit can accomplish among these wandering sheep He sees around Him. He longs for help to have them properly cared for. He therefore tells His disciples to begin to pray.

When they have taken over the work from Him on earth, they are to make this one of their chief petitions in prayer—that the Lord of the harvest Himself would send laborers into His harvest. And since He entrusts them with continuing His work and makes it to a large extent dependent on them, He gives them authority to apply to Him for the laborers they will need and makes the supply dependent on their prayer.

NEED FOR LABORERS

How little Christians really feet and mourn the need for laborers in the fields of the world, so ripe for the harvest. How little they believe that our labor supply depends on prayer and that prayer will really provide "as many as he needs." The lack of laborers is known and discussed. Efforts are sometimes made to supply the need. But how little the burden of the sheep wandering without a Shepherd is really translated into faith that the Lord of the harvest *will* send forth the laborers in answer to prayer. Without this prayer, fields ready for reaping will be left to perish.

The Lord has surrendered His work to His Church. He has made himself dependent on them as His body, through whom His work must be done. The power that the Lord gives His people to exercise in heaven and earth is real. *The number of laborers and the measure of the harvest does actually depend on their prayer.*

Two Reasons Why We Do Not Obey the Master

Why do we not obey the Master's instruction more heartily and cry more earnestly for laborers? There are two reasons.

One reason is that we do not have the compassion of Jesus that gave rise to this request for prayer. To live entirely for God's glory in their relationships with others, believers must learn to love their neighbors as themselves.[3] The second commandment to God's redeemed ones is that they accept those who are perishing as the charge entrusted to them by their Lord. Accept them not only as a field of labor, but as the objects of loving care and interest. Do this, and soon compassion towards the hopelessly perishing will touch your heart, and your cry will ascend with a new sincerity.

The other reason for the neglect of the command is that we believe too little in the power of prayer to bring about definite results. We do not live close enough to God to be capable of the confidence that He will answer. We have not surrendered entirely to His service and kingdom. But our lack of faith will be overcome as we plead for help. Let us pray for a life in union with Christ, so that His compassion streams into us and His Spirit assures us that our prayer is heard.

Desire for an Increase in Laborers

There will first be a desire for an increase in the number of those entirely given up to the service of God. That there are times when no one can be found for the service of the Master as ministers, missionaries, or teachers of God's Word is a terrible blot upon the Church of Christ. As God's children make this a matter of supplication in their own circles or churches, laborers will be given.

The Lord Jesus is now Lord of the harvest. He has been exalted to bestow the gifts of the Spirit. He wants to make gifts of people filled with the Spirit. But His supply and distribution of these gifts depend on the cooperation of the Church with Him. Prayer will lead to such cooperation and will stir those praying to believe that they will find the men and women who are needed—and the means necessary for the work.

The other blessing will be equally great. Every believer is a laborer. As God's children, we have been redeemed for service and have our work waiting. It must be our prayer that the Lord would fill all His people with the spirit of devotion, so that no one may be found standing idle in the vineyard.

Wherever there is a complaint about the lack of fit helpers for God's work, prayer has the promise of a supply. God is always ready and able to provide. It may take time and importunity, but Christ's command to ask the Lord of the harvest is the pledge that the prayer will be heard. "I say to you, . . . he will rise and give him as many as he needs."[4]

POWER TO SECURE LABORERS

This power to provide for the needs of the world and secure the servants for God's work has been given to us in prayer. The Lord of the harvest will hear. Christ who taught us to pray this way will support the prayers offered in His Name and interest. Let us set apart time and give all of ourselves to this part of our intercessory work.

Doing such will lead us into the fellowship of that compassionate heart of His that led Him to call for our prayers. It will give us the insight of our royal position as children of the King, whose will counts for something with the great God in the advancement of His kingdom. We will feel that we really are God's co-workers on earth, that we have earnestly been entrusted with a share in His work. We will become partakers in the work of the soul. But we will also share in the satisfaction of the soul as we learn how, in answer to prayer, blessing has been given that otherwise would not have come.

LORD, TEACH US TO PRAY

Blessed Lord! Once again You have given us another wondrous lesson to learn. We humbly ask that You let us see these spiritual realities. There is a large harvest that is perishing as it waits for sleepy disciples to give the signal for laborers to come. Lord, teach us to view it with a heart full of compassion and pity. There are so few laborers, Lord.

Show us what terrible sin the lack of prayer and faith is, considering there is a Lord of the harvest so able and ready to send them forth. Show us how God does indeed wait for the prayer to which He has promised an answer. We are the disciples to whom the commission to pray has been given.

Lord, show us how You can breathe your Spirit into us, so that Your compassion and the faith in Your promise will rouse us to unceasing, prevailing, prayer.

O Lord! We cannot understand how You can entrust such work and give such power to disciples so slothful and unfaithful. We thank You for all those whom You are teaching day and night to cry for laborers to be sent.

Lord, breathe your Spirit into all Your children. Let them learn to live only for the kingdom and glory of their Lord and become fully awake to the faith in what their prayer can accomplish. Fill our hearts with the assurance that prayer offered in living faith in the living God will bring certain and abundant answer. Amen.

NOTES ON LESSON EIGHT

[1] Matthew 9:37-38
[2] Matthew 9:36
[3] Mark 12:31
[4] Luke 11:8

PERSONAL NOTES

_____

_____

_____

_____

_____

_____

_____

_____

_____

_____

_____

_____

_____

_____

LESSON 9

PRAYER MUST BE SPECIFIC

*Then Jesus said to him, "What do you
want Me to do for you?"*[1]

The blind beggar had been crying out loud
repeatedly, "Son of David, have mercy on me!"[2] The
cry had reached the ear of the Lord. He knew what the
man wanted and was ready to grant it to him. But before
He did it, He asked him, *"What do you want* me to do
for you?"* He wanted to hear not only the general
petition for mercy, but the distinct expression of what
the man's desire was that day. Until he verbalized it,
he was not healed.

There are still petitioners to whom the Lord puts
the same question, and who cannot get the aid they need
until they answer that question. Our prayers must *be a
distinct expression of definite need*, not a vague appeal
to His mercy or an indefinite cry for blessing. It is not

that His loving heart does not understand or is not ready to hear our cry. Rather, Christ desires such definite prayer for our own sakes because it teaches us to know our own needs better. Time, thought, and self-scrutiny are required to find out what our greatest need really is. Our desires are put to the test to see whether they are honest and real and are according to God's Word, and whether we really believe we will receive the things we ask. Such reflective prayer helps us to wait for the special answer and to mark it when it comes.

VAGUE AND POINTLESS PRAYING

So much of our praying is vague and pointless. Some cry for mercy, but do not take the trouble to know exactly why they want it. Others ask to be delivered from sin, but do not name any sin from which a deliverance can be claimed. Still others pray for God's blessing on those around them—or the outpouring of God's Spirit on their land or on the world—and yet have no special field where they can wait and expect to see the answer. To everyone the Lord says, in essence, "What do you *really* want, and what do you *really* expect Me to do?"

Christian have only limited power. Just as we must have our own specific field of labor in which to serve God, we must also make our prayers specific. Each of us have our own circle, family, friends, and neighbors. If we were to take one or more of these by name, we would find ourselves entering the training school of faith that leads to personal dealing with our God. When we have faithfully claimed and received answers in such distinct matters, our more general prayers will be believing and effectual. Not many prayers will reach the mark if we just pour out our hearts in a multitude of petitions, without taking time to see whether every petition is sent with the purpose and expectation of getting an answer.

Bow before the Lord with silence in your soul and ask such questions as these:

- What is really my desire?
- Do I desire it in faith, expecting to receive an answer?
- Am I ready to present it to the Father and leave it there in His hands?
- Is there agreement between God and me that I will get an answer?
- Am I in agreement with myself—spirit, soul, and body—that I will get an answer?

We should learn to pray in such a way that God will see, and we will know what we really expect.

The Lord warns us against the vain repetitions of the Gentiles, who expect to be heard because they pray so much.[3]   We often hear prayers of great earnestness and fervor, in which a multitude of petitions are poured forth. The Savior would undoubtedly have to respond to some of them by asking, "What *do* you want?"

Two Kinds of Letters

If I were in a foreign country on business for my father or mother, I would certainly write two different sorts of letters home. There will be family letters with typical affectionate expressions in them, and there will be business letters containing orders for what I need. They may also be letters in which both are found. The answers will correspond to the letters.

73

To each sentence of the letters containing the family news I do not expect a special answer. But for each order I send I am confident of an answer regarding the forwarding of the desired article.

In our dealings with God, the business element must be present. Our expressions of need, sin, love, faith, and consecration must be accompanied by an explicit statement of *exactly* what we are asking for and *exactly* what we expect to receive. In response, the Father loves to give us a token of His approval and acceptance.

Wishing But Not Willing

But the word of the Master teaches us more. He does not say, "What does thou *wish?*" but "What does thou *will?*"[4] One often wishes for a thing without willing it. I wish to have a certain article but the price is too high, so I decide not to take it. I *wish,* but do not *will* to have it. The lazy man wishes to be rich, but does not will it. Many people wish to be saved, but perish because they do not will it.

The will rules the whole heart and life. If I really will to have something that is within my reach, I do not rest until I have it. When Jesus asks us, "What wilt thou?" He asks whether it is our intention to get what we ask for at any price, however great the sacrifice. Do you really will to have it enough to pray continuously until He hears you, no matter how long it takes? Many prayers are wishes sent up for a short time and then forgotten. And many are sent up year after year as a matter of duty, while we complacently wait without the answer.

LEAVING THE ANSWER TO GOD

One may ask if it would not be better to make our wishes known to God, leaving it to Him to decide what is best, without our seeking to assert our wills. The answer is, *by no means.—definitely not.* The prayer of faith that Jesus sought to teach His disciples does not simply proclaim its desire and then leave the decision to God. That would be the prayer of submission for cases in which we cannot know God's will. But the prayer of faith, finding God's will in some promise of the Word, pleads for that promise until it comes.

In Matthew 9:28, Jesus said to the blind man, *"Do you believe that I am able to do this?"* In Mark 10:51 He said, *"What do you want Me to do for you?"* In both cases He said that faith had saved them.[5] And He said to the Syrophenician woman,[6] too, "Great is *thy faith: be* it unto thee even as thou wilt."[7] Faith is nothing but the purpose of the will resting on God's Word and saying, "I must have it." *To believe truly is to will firmly.*

SUBMISSION TO GOD

Such a will is not at variance with our dependence on God and our submission to Him. Rather, it is the true submission that honors God. It is only when God's children have yielded their own will in entire surrender to the Father that they receive from Him the liberty and power to will what they desire.

Once we accept the will of God, as revealed through the Word and the Spirit, as our will, too, then it is the desire of God that we use our renewed will in His service.

75

The Will Is the Highest Power of the Soul

Because the will is the highest power of the soul, grace desires above everything to sanctify and restore this will to full and free exercise, for it is one of the chief traits of God's image. God's child is like a son or daughter who live only for their father's interest, seek their father's will rather than their own, and are trusted by the father with his business. God speaks to them in all truth, "What wilt thou?"

It is often spiritual sloth that—under the appearance of humility—professes to have no will. It fears the trouble of searching for the will of God, or, when found, the struggle of claiming it in faith. *True humility is always accompanied by strong faith.* Seeking to know only the will of God, that faith then boldly claims the fulfillment of the promise, "Ye shall ask what ye will, and it shall be done unto you."[8]

Lord, Teach Us to Pray

Lord Jesus! Teach me to pray with all my heart and strength that there may be no doubt with You or with me about what I have asked. I want to know what I desire so well that as my petitions are being recorded in heaven, I can also record them here on earth and note each answer as it comes. Make my faith in what Your Word has promised so clear that the Spirit may work within me the liberty to will that it will come.

Lord! Renew, strengthen, and sanctify my entire will for the work of effectual prayer.

Blessed Savior! I pray that You reveal to me the wonderful grace You show us, the grace that asks us to say what we desire and then promises to do it.

Son of God! I cannot fully understand it. I can only believe that You have indeed redeemed us wholly for Yourself, and that You want to mold our wills, making them Your most efficient servant.

Lord! I unreservedly yield my will to You as the channel through which Your Spirit is to rule my whole being. Let Him take possession of it, lead it into the truth of Your promises, and make it so strong in prayer that I may always hear Your voice saying, "Great is thy faith: be it unto thee even as thou wilt." Amen.

Notes on Lesson Nine

[1] Mark 10:51, Luke 18:41

[2] Mark 10:48, Luke 18:39

[3] Matthew 6:7

[4] Paraphrase of KJV version of Mark 10:51 and Luke 18:41, which read, "What wilt thou that I shall do unto thee?"

[5] Matthew 9:29, Mark 10:52

[6] Mark refers to her as a Syrophenician woman, Matthew calls her a Canaanite woman, or woman from Canaan, depending on Bible version.

[7] Matthew 15:28, KJV

[8] John 15:7, KJV

PERSONAL NOTES

LESSON 10

THE FAITH THAT TAKES

*Therefore I say unto you, All things
whatsoever you pray and ask for, believe
that you have received them [see
Endnote¹] and you shall have them [see
Endnote²].*

What a promise! It is so large, so divine, that our
little hearts cannot comprehend it. In every possible
way we seek to limit it to what we think is safe or
probable. We don't allow it to come in just as Jesus
gave it to us with its quickening power and energy. If
we would allow it, that promise would enlarge our
hearts to receive all of what His love and power are
really ready to do for us.

Faith is very far from being a mere conviction of
the truth of God's Word or a conclusion drawn from
certain premises. It is the [inner] ear that has heard God
say what He will do, and the [inner] eye that has seen
Him doing it. Therefore, where there is true faith it is

impossible for the answer not to come. We must but do this one thing that He asks of us as we pray: *Believe that you have received.* He will see to it that He does the thing He has promised: *you shall have them.*

The essence of Solomon's prayer is, "Praise be to the LORD, the God of Israel, who *with his hands has fulfilled* what *he promised with his mouth* to my father David."[3] This should be the essence of all true prayer. It is the joyful adoration of a God whose *hands* always secure the fulfillment of what His *mouth* has promised [see Endnote[4]]. Let us in this spirit listen to the promise Jesus gives because each part of it has a divine message.

ALL THINGS WHATSOEVER

"All things whatsoever." From the first word our human wisdom begins to doubt and say, *this can't possibly be literally true.* But if it is not, why did the Master say it? He used the very strongest expression He could find: "all things whatsoever." And He said it more than once "If you can believe, *all things* are possible to him who believes."[5] "If you have faith as a mustard seed, . . . *nothing* will be impossible for you."[6]

Faith is completely the work of God's Spirit through His Word in the prepared heart of the believing disciple. It is impossible for the fulfillment not to come, because faith is the pledge and forerunner of the coming answer.[7]

BELIEVE THAT YOU HAVE RECEIVED

"All things whatsoever you pray and ask for, *believe that you have received.*" The tendency of human reason is to intervene here with certain qualifiers, such as, "if expedient," "if according to God's will," to break the force of a statement that appears dangerous. Beware of dealing this way with the Master's words. His promise is most literally true. He wants His frequently repeated "all things" to enter our hearts and reveal how mighty the power of faith is.

The head truly calls the members of His body to share His power with Him. Our Father places His power at the disposal of the child who completely trusts Him. Faith gets its food and strength from the "all things" of Christ's promise. As we weaken it, we weaken faith.

The *whatsoever is* unconditional except for what is implied in believing. Before we can believe, *we must find out and know what God's will is*. Believing is the exercise of a soul surrendered to the influence of the Word and the Spirit. Once we do believe, nothing is impossible. Let us pray that we do not limit Christ's "all things" with what we think is possible. His "whatsoever" alone should determine the boundaries of our hope and faith. It is seed-word that we should take just as He gives it and plant it in our hearts. It will germinate and take root, filling our lives with its fullness and bearing abundant fruit.

WHATSOEVER *YOU PRAY AND ASK FOR*

"All things whatsoever *you pray and ask for*." It is in prayer that these "all things" are to be brought to God. The faith that received them is the fruit of the prayer. There must be a certain amount of faith before there can be prayer, but greater faith is the result of prayer. In the personal presence of the Savior and in conversation with Him, faith rises to grasp what at first appeared too high.

Through prayer we hold up our desires to the light of God's holy will, our motives are tested, and proof is given whether we are indeed asking in the name of Jesus and only for the glory of God. The leading of the Spirit shows us whether we are asking for the right thing and in the right spirit. The weakness of our faith becomes obvious as we pray. But we are encouraged to say to the Father that we do believe and that we prove the reality of our faith by the confidence with which we persevere.

It is in prayer that Jesus teaches and inspires faith. Whoever waits to pray, or loses heart in prayer because they do not feel the faith needed to get an answer, will never learn that faith. Whoever begins to pray and ask will find the Spirit of faith is given nowhere so surely as at the foot of the throne.

BELIEVE THAT YOU HAVE RECEIVED

"*Believe* that you have received." Clearly we are to believe that we receive the very things we ask. The Savior does not say that the Father may give us something else because He knows what is best. The very mountain that faith wants to remove is cast into the sea.[8]

There is one kind of prayer in which we make known our request in everything, and the reward is the sweet peace of God in our hearts and minds.[9] This is the prayer of trust. It makes reference to the countless desires of daily life that we cannot find out if God will give. We leave it to Him to decide whether or not to give, as He knows best.

But the prayer of faith in which Jesus speaks is something higher and different. Nothing honors the Father like the faith that is assured that He will do what He has said in giving us whatever we ask. Such faith takes its stand on the promise delivered by the Spirit. It knows most certainly that it receives exactly what it asks, whether in the greater interest of the Master's work or in the lesser concerns of daily life. Notice how clearly the Lord states this in Mark 11:23: "whoever . . . does not doubt in his heart, but believes that those things he says will be done, he will have whatever he says." This is the blessing of the prayer of faith of which Jesus speaks.

Believe That You *Have Received*

"Believe that you *have received.*" This word of central importance is too often misunderstood. Believe that you have received what you're asking for *now,* while praying. You may not actually see it manifested until later. But now, without seeing it, you are to believe that it has *already been given to you* by the Father in heaven. Receiving or accepting an answer to prayer is just like receiving or accepting Jesus. It is a spiritual thing, an act of faith separate from all feeling.

When I go to Jesus, asking Him for forgiveness for a sin, I believe He is in heaven for just that purpose, and I accept His forgiveness. In the same way, when I go to God asking for any special gift that is *according to His Word,* I must believe that what I desire is mine. I believe that I have it, I hold it in faith, and I thank God that it's mine. "If we know that He hears us— whatever we ask—we know that we have what we asked of Him."[10]

AND YE SHALL HAVE THEM

"And ye shall have them." The gift that we first hold in faith as ours from heaven will become ours in personal experience. But will it be necessary to pray longer once we know we have been heard and have received what we asked? Additional prayer will not be necessary when the blessing is on its way. In these cases we should maintain our confidence, proving our faith by praising God for what we have received, even though we haven't experienced it yet.

There are other cases, however, in which faith needs to be further tried and strengthened in persevering prayer. Only God knows when everything is fully ripe for the manifestation of the blessing that has been given to faith.

Elijah knew for certain that rain would come. God had promised it, and yet he had to pray seven times. That prayer was not just for show. It was an intense spiritual reality both in the heart of Elijah as he lay there pleading and in heaven where it had its effectual work to do. It is through faith land *patience* we inherit the promises.[11]

Faith says most confidently, "I have received it." [Not *will* receive, *have* received.] Patience perseveres in prayer until the gift bestowed in heaven is seen on earth. "Believe that *you have received* them, and *you shall have* them." Between the *have received* in heaven, and the *shall have* of earth, the key word *is believe.* Believing praise and prayer is the link. Remember that it is Jesus who said this.

HEAVEN OPENED TO US

As we see heaven opened to us and the Father on the throne offering to give us whatever we ask for in faith, we are ashamed that we have so little availed ourselves of the privilege. We feel afraid that our feeble faith will still not be able to grasp what is so clearly placed within our reach. One thing must make us strong and full of hope—*It is Jesus who brought us this message from the Father.*

Jesus lived the life of faith and prayer when He was on earth. When the disciples expressed their surprise at what He had done to the fig tree, He told them that the very same life He led could be theirs. They could command not only the fig tree, but the very mountain, and they would obey.

CHRIST IS EVERYTHING

In us Christ is everything now that He was on earth. He really gives everything He teaches. He is the author and perfecter [finisher] of our faith.[12] He gives the spirit of faith.[13]

Don't be afraid that such faith is not meant for us. Meant for every child of the Father, it is within the reach of all who will be childlike, yielding themselves to the Father's will and love, and trusting the Father's Word and power.

HAVE COURAGE AND BELIEVE

Have courage! This word comes through Jesus, who is God's son and your brother. Let your answer be, "Yes, blessed Lord, I do believe Your Word that I receive whatever I ask."

LORD, TEACH US TO PRAY

Blessed Lord! The Father sent You to show us all His love and all the treasures of blessing that love is waiting to bestow.

Lord! You've given us such abundant promises concerning our liberty in prayer. We are ashamed that our poor hearts have accepted so little of it. It has simply seemed too much for us to believe.

Lord! Teach us to take and keep and use Your precious Word: "All things whatsoever you pray and ask for, believe that you have received them."

Blessed Jesus! It is in You that our faith must be rooted if it is to grow strong. Your work has completely freed us from the power of sin and has opened the way to the Father. Your love is longing to bring us into the full fellowship of Your glory and power. Your Spirit is constantly drawing us into a life of perfect faith and confidence. We are sure that through Your teaching we will learn to pray the prayer of faith. You will train us to pray so that we will believe that we really have what we ask for.

Lord! Teach me to know and trust and love You in such a way that I live and dwell in You. Through You, may all my prayers rise up and go before God, and may my soul have the assurance that I am heard. Amen.

NOTES ON LESSON TEN

[1] The KJV and NKJV read, "believe that you receive," but the NRSV, NIV, and NASB has it in the

past tense, "believe that you have received," as does *The Interlinear Greek-English New Testament*. The difference though small in human words is vast in divine principle.

² Mark 11:24 — The exact text of the author's quotation could not be found in any current Bible version, but it was left intact, except for changing *ye* to *you*, because to change it would require too many changes in the lesson text, which has been left in its original version to agree with the quotation.

³ 2 Chronicles 6:4

⁴ Note how well this harmonizes with Paul's statement about Abraham in Romans 4:20-21—"He did not waver at the promise of God through unbelief, but was strengthened in faith, [while] giving glory to God, and being fully convinced that what He had promised He was also able to perform."

⁵ Mark 9:23

⁶ Matthew 17:20

⁷ Hebrews 11:1

⁸ Mark 11:23

⁹ Philippians 4:7

¹⁰ 1 John 5:15

¹¹ Hebrews 6:12

¹² Hebrews 12:2

¹³ 2 Corinthians 4:13

Personal Notes

LESSON 11

THE SECRET OF BELIEVING PRAYER

So Jesus answered and said to them,
"Have faith in God.
"For assuredly, I say to you, whoever
says to this mountain, 'Be removed and
be cast into the sea,' and does not doubt
in his heart, but believes that those things
he says will be done, he will have
whatever he says."[1]

Answer to prayer is one of the most wonderful lessons in all the Scriptures. In many hearts it must raise the question, "How can I ever attain the faith that knows it receives everything it asks for?" It is this question our Lord will answer in this lesson.

Before He gave that wonderful promise to His disciples, Christ shows where faith in the answer to prayer originates and finds its strength. *Have faith in God.* This faith precedes the faith in the promise of an answer to prayer. The power to believe *a promise* depends entirely on faith in *the promiser*. Trust in the person gives rise to trust in what he or she says.

We must live and associate with God in personal, loving, communication. God Himself should be everything to us. His Holy presence is revealed where our whole being is opened and exposed to His mighty influence. There the capacity for believing His promises will be developed.

WHAT FAITH REALLY IS

The connection between faith in God and faith in His promise will become clear to us if we consider what faith really is. It is often compared to the hand or the mouth, by which we take and use what is given to us. But it is important that we understand that faith is also the ear by which we hear what is promised and the eye by which we see what is offered. The power to take depends on this.

I must *hear* the person who gives me the promise because the very tone of their voice gives me courage to believe. I must *see* the person because the light of their face melts all my qualms about my right to take, The value of the promise depends on the promiser. It is on my knowledge of what the promiser is that faith in the promise depends.

FAITH IS THE EYE

Faith is the eye. For this reason Jesus says, *Have faith in God,* before He gives the wonderful prayer-promise. Let your [inner] eye be open to the living God. Through this eye we yield ourselves to God's influence. Just allow it to enter and leave its impression on our minds.

Believing God is simply looking at God and what He is, and allowing Him to reveal His presence to us. Give Him time and completely yield to Him, receiving and rejoicing in His love. Faith is the eye through which the light of God's presence and the vigor of His power stream into the soul. As that which I see lives in me, so by faith God lives in me, too.

FAITH IS THE EAR

Faith is also the ear through which the voice of God is always heard. The Father speaks to us through the Holy Spirit. The Son is the Word[2] —the substance of what God says—and the Spirit is the living voice.

The children of God need this secret voice from heaven to guide them[3] and teach them,[4] as it [He] taught Jesus what to say and what to do. An ear opened towards God is a believing heart that waits to hear what He says.

The words of God will be not only the words of a book, they will be spirit, truth, life, and power. They will make mere thoughts come to life. Through this opened ear, the soul abides under the influence of the life and power of God Himself. As His words enter the mind, dwelling and working there, through faith God enters the heart, dwelling and working there.

FAITH IN FULL USE

When faith is in full use as eye and ear—the faculties of the soul by which we see and hear God—

then it will be able to exercise its full power as hand and mouth—the faculties by which we take God and His blessings. The power of reception will depend entirely on the power of spiritual perception.

For this reason, before Jesus gave the promise that God would answer believing prayer, He said, "Have faith in God." Faith is simply surrender. I yield myself to the suggestions I hear. By faith *I yield myself to the living* God. His glory and love fill my heart and have mastery over my life. I give myself up to the influence of a friend who makes me a promise and become linked to that person by it. When we enter into living fellowship with *God Himself,* in a faith that always sees and hears Him, it becomes easy and natural to believe His promise regarding prayer.

FAITH IN THE PROMISE

Faith in the promise is the fruit of faith in the promiser. The prayer of faith is rooted in the life of faith. And in this way the faith that prays effectively is indeed a gift of God. It is not something He bestows or infuses all at once, but is far deeper and truer. It is the blessed disposition or habit of soul that grows up in us through a life of communion with Him.

Surely for one who knows our Father well and lives in constant close communion with Him, it is a simple thing to believe the promise that He will do what His child wishes.

UNDERSTANDING THE FAITH CONNECTION

Because very many of God's children do not understand this connection between the life of faith and the prayer of faith, their experience of the power of prayer is limited. Sincerely desiring to obtain an answer from God, they concentrate wholeheartedly on the promise and try their utmost to grasp that promise in faith. When they do not succeed, they are ready to give up hope. The promise is true, but it is beyond their power to accept it in faith.

Listen to the lesson Jesus teaches us—*Have faith in God, the living God.* Let faith focus on God more than on the thing promised, because it is His love, His power, His living presence that will awaken and work the faith. To someone asking to develop more strength in their hands and arms, a physician would say that their whole constitution must be built up. So the cure of feeble faith can be found only in the invigoration of our whole spiritual lives through communication with God.

Learn to believe in God, to hold on to God, and to let God take possession of your life. It will then become easy to grasp the promise. Whoever knows and trusts God finds it easy to also trust the promise.

Special Revelation From God

Note how distinctly this comes out in former saints—every exhibition of the power of faith was the fruit of a special revelation from God. We see it in Abraham [when still called Abram]:

> After this, the word of the LORD came to Abram in a vision: "Do not be afraid, Abram. I am your shield . . . He took him outside and *said, . . .* and Abram believed the LORD.[5]

And later again:

> The LORD appeared to him
> [Abram] and *said*, "I am God Almighty"
> . . . Abram fell facedown, and God *said*
> to him, "As for me, this is my covenant
> with you."[6]

It was the revelation of God Himself that gave the promise its living power to enter the heart and cultivate the faith. Because they knew God, the men and women of faith could not do anything but trust His promise. God's promise will be to us what God himself is.

Those who walk before the Lord and fall on their face to listen while the living God speaks to them will receive the promise. We have God's promises in the Bible with full liberty to claim them. Our spiritual power depends on *God Himself speaking those promises to us. He speaks* to *those who walk and live with Him.*

FAITH IN GOD

Therefore, have faith in God. Let faith be all eyes and ears. Surrender to God and let Him make His full impression on you, revealing Himself fully in your soul. Consider it a blessing of prayer that you can exercise faith in God as the living almighty God who is waiting to give us the good pleasure of His will and faith with power. Regard Him as the God of love, whose delight it is to bless and impart His love.

In such faithful worship of God, the power will speedily come to believe the promise, too. "Whatever you ask for in prayer, believe that you have received it."[7] Make God your own through faith—the promise will become yours, also.

94

A Precious Lesson

Christ is teaching us a precious lesson. We seek God's gifts, but God wants to give us Himself first. We think of prayer as the means of extracting good gifts from heaven, and we think of Christ as the means to draw ourselves up to God. We want to stand at the door and cry. Christ wants us to enter in and realize that we are friends and children. Accept His teaching.

Let every experience of the weakness of our faith incite us to have and exercise more faith in the living God, and in such faith to yield ourselves to Him. A heart full of God has power for the prayer of faith. Faith in God fosters faith in the promise, including the promise of an answer to prayer.

Therefore, child of God, take time to bow before *Him* and wait for *Him* to reveal *Himself.* Take time to let your soul exercise and express its faith in the infinite one in holy worship. As He shares himself with and takes possession of you, the prayer of faith will crown your faith in God.

Lord, Teach Us to Pray

O my God! I do believe in you. I believe you are the Father, infinite in Your love and power. As the Son, You are my redeemer and my life. And as the Holy Spirit, You are my comforter, my guide, and my strength. I have faith that You will share everything You are with me and that You will do everything You promise.

Lord Jesus! Increase my faith.[8] Teach me to take time to wait and worship in God's Holy presence until my faith absorbs everything there is in Him

95

for me. Let my faith see Him as the fountain of all life, working with almighty strength to accomplish His will in the world and in me. Let me see Him in His love longing to meet and fulfill my desires. Let faith take possession of my heart and life to the extent that through it God may dwell there.

Lord Jesus, help me! I want with my whole heart to believe in God. Fill me every moment with faith in God.

O my Blessed Savior! How can your Church glorify You and fulfill the work of intercession through which Your kingdom will come unless our whole lives consist of faith in God.

Blessed Lord! Speak Your Word, "Have faith in God," into the depths of our souls. Amen.

NOTES ON LESSON ELEVEN

[1] Mark 11:22-23
[2] John 1:1
[3] Romans 8:14, Galatians 5:18
[4] Luke 12:12; John 14:26; Acts 1:2, 13:2
[5] Genesis 15:1, 5, 6
[6] Genesis 17:1, 3, 4
[7] Mark 11:24, NIV
[8] Luke 17:5

PERSONAL NOTES

_____

_____

LESSON 12

PRAYER AND FASTING

*Then the disciples came to Jesus privately
and said, "Why could we not cast it out?"
So Jesus said to them, "Because of your
unbelief; for assuredly, I say to you, if
you have faith as a mustard seed, you will
say to this mountain, 'Move from here to
there,' and it will move; and nothing will
be impossible for you.
"However, this kind does not go out
except by prayer and fasting."* [1]

When the disciples saw Jesus cast the evil spirit
out of the epileptic whom "they could not cure,"[2] they
asked the Master why they had failed. He had already
given them "authority over unclean spirits, to cast them
out, and to cure every disease and every sickness."[3]
They had often exercised that power,[4] and joyfully told
how the devils were subject to them.[5] And yet now,
while He was on the Mount, they had utterly failed.

97

Christ's casting the evil spirit out proved that there had been nothing in the will of God or in the nature of the case to make the miracle impossible. From their expression, "Why could we not?" it is evident that the disciples had wanted and tried to cast the spirit out. They had probably called upon it, using the Master's name. But their efforts had been in vain. They had been put to shame in front of the crowd.

UNBELIEF

Christ's answer was direct and plain, "Because of your unbelief." Christ's success was not a result of His having a special power to which the disciples had no access. He had so often taught them that there is one power—the power of faith—to which, in the kingdom of darkness as in the kingdom of God, everything must bow. In the spiritual world, failure has only one cause— lack of faith. Faith is the one condition on which all divine power can enter us and work through us. It is the sensitivity of our will yielded to and molded by the will of God.

The power the disciples had received to cast out devils did not belong to them as a permanent gift or possession. The power was in Christ, to be received, held, and used by faith alone, living faith in Him. Had they been full of faith *in Him* as Lord and conqueror in the spirit world, had they been full of faith *in Him* as having given them authority to cast out in His name, their faith would have given them the victory. "Because of your unbelief" was, for all time, the Master's explanation and reproof of impotence and failure in His Church.

CAUSE OF DEFICIENT FAITH

Such a deficiency of faith must have a cause. The disciples may have asked, "Why couldn't we believe? Our faith has cast out devils before this. Why did we fail in believing this time?" The Master answers them before they can ask, "this kind does not go out except by prayer and fasting."

Though faith is the simplest exercise of the spiritual life, it is also the highest. The spirit must yield itself in perfect receptivity to God's Spirit and become strengthened for this activity. Such faith depends entirely on the state of the spiritual life. Only when this is strong and in good health—when the Spirit of God has total influence in our lives—does faith have the power to do its mighty deeds.

PRAYER AND FASTING

Therefore Jesus adds, "However, this kind does not go out except by prayer and fasting." The faith that can overcome stubborn resistance such as you have just seen in this evil spirit, Jesus tells them, is not possible except for those living in very close fellowship with God and in very special separation from the world—in prayer and fasting.

So He teaches us two lessons of deep importance in regard to prayer. The first is that faith needs a life of prayer in which to grow and keep strong. The second is that prayer needs fasting for its full and perfect development.

FIRST LESSON—THERE IS A CLOSE UNION BETWEEN FAITH AND PRAYER

In all the different parts of the spiritual life there is a close union between unceasing action and reaction, so that each may be both cause and effect. Thus it is with faith. There can be no true prayer without faith— some measure of faith must precede prayer. And yet prayer is also the way to more faith. No higher degrees of faith can be obtained except through much prayer. This is the lesson Jesus teaches here.

Nothing needs to grow as much as our faith. "Your faith grows exceedingly"[6] Paul said to the church at Thessalonica. When Jesus spoke the words, "According to your faith will it be done to you,"[7] He announced the law of the kingdom, which tells us that different people have different degrees of faith, that one person may have varying degrees, and that the amount of faith will always determine the amount of one's power and blessing.

WHERE AND HOW OUR FAITH GROWS

If we want to know where and how our faith is to grow, the Master points us to the throne of God. It is in prayer, exercising one's faith in fellowship with the living God, that faith can increase. Faith can only live by feeding on what is divine, on God Himself.

It is in the adoring worship of God—the waiting on Him and for Him in the deep silence of a soul yielding itself so God will reveal Himself—that the capacity for knowing and trusting God will be developed. As we take His Word from the Blessed Book and ask Him to speak it to us with His living, loving, voice, the power to believe and receive the Word as God's own word to us will emerge in us.

It is in prayer, in living contact with God in living faith, that faith will become strong in us. Many Christians cannot understand, nor do they feel the need, of spending hours with God. But the Master says, and the experience of His people has confirmed, that people of strong faith are people of much prayer.

Have Faith in God

This brings us back again to the lesson we learned when Jesus, before telling us to believe that we receive what we ask for, first said, "Have faith in God." It is God—the living God—into whom our faith must strike its roots deeply and broadly. Then it will be strong enough to remove mountains and cast out devils. "If you have faith . . . nothing will be impossible for you."

If we could only give ourselves up to the work God has for us in the world. As we came into contact with the mountains and the devils that are to be cast away and cast out, we would soon comprehend how much we need great faith and prayer. They alone are the soil in which faith can be cultivated. *Christ Jesus is our life*[8] *and the life of our faith.* It is His life in us that makes us strong and ready to believe. The dying to self that much prayer implies, allows a closer union to Christ in which the spirit of faith will come in power. *Faith needs prayer* for its full growth.

Second Lesson—Prayer Needs Fasting

Because of the often negative effect of the body upon the spirit, *prayer needs fasting* for its full growth.

Prayer is the one hand with which we grasp the invisible. Fasting is the other hand, the one with which we let go of the visible. In nothing are we more closely connected with the world of sense than in our need and enjoyment of food. It was with fruit that the woman and man were tempted and fell in the Garden of Eden. It was with bread that Jesus was tempted in the wilderness. But He triumphed in fasting.

The body has been redeemed to be a temple of the Holy Spirit. In body as well as spirit, Scripture says, we are to glorify God in eating and drinking.[9] There are many Christians to whom this eating for the glory of God has not yet become a spiritual reality. The first thought suggested by Jesus' words in regard to fasting and prayer is that only in a life of moderation and self-denial will there be sufficient heart and strength to pray much.

Sorrow and anxiety cannot eat, but joy celebrates its feasts with eating and drinking. There may come times of intense desire, when it is strongly felt how the body and its appetites still hinder the spirit in its battle with the powers of darkness. A need is felt to keep it subdued. We are creatures of the senses. Our minds are helped by what comes to us in concrete form.

Fasting helps to express, to deepen, and to confirm the resolution that we are ready to sacrifice anything, even ourselves, to attain the kingdom of God. And Jesus, who Himself fasted and sacrificed, knows to value, accept, and reward with spiritual power the soul that is thus ready to give up everything for Him and His kingdom.

PRAYER REACHES OUT FOR GOD

Prayer is reaching out for God and the unseen. Fasting is letting go of everything that can be seen and touched. Some Christians imagine that everything that is not positively forbidden and sinful is permissible to them. So they try to retain as much as possible of this world with its property, its literature, and its enjoyments. The truly consecrated soul, however, is like a soldier who carries only what is needed for battle.

Once free of all unnecessary weight, a person is easily capable of combating sin. Afraid of becoming entangling with the affairs of a worldly life, the person then tries to lead a Nazarite life as one specially set apart for the Lord and His service. Without such voluntary separation, even from what is lawful, no one will attain power in prayer. Such power comes only through fasting and prayer.

ACCEPT THE LESSONS OF CHRIST

You have asked the Master to teach you to pray, so come now and accept His lessons. He tells you that prayer is the path to faith—strong faith that can cast out devils. He tells you: "If you have faith . . . nothing will be impossible for you." Let this glorious promise encourage you to pray much. Isn't the prize worth the price?

Give up everything to follow Christ in the path He opens to us. Pray much. Fast if you need to. Do anything you must so neither the body nor the world can hinder you in the great life-work He has for us—talking to God in prayer, so that we may become people of faith whom He can use in His work of saving the world.

LORD, TEACH US TO PRAY

O Lord Jesus! How continually You must reprimand us for our unbelief. Our terrible inability to trust our Father and His promises must appear quite strange to You.

Lord! Let Your words, "Because of your unbelief," sink into the very depths of our hearts and reveal how much of the sin and suffering around us is our fault. Then teach us, Blessed Lord, that faith can be gained and learned in the prayer and fasting that brings us into living fellowship with You and the Father.

O Savior! You are the author and the finisher of our faith.[10] Teach us what it means to let You live in us by Your Holy Spirit.

Lord! Our efforts and prayers for grace to believe have been so ineffective. We know it is because we want You to give us strength in ourselves.

Holy Christ! Teach us the mystery of Your life in us—how You, by Your Spirit, live the life of faith in us, insuring that our faith will not fail. Make our faith a part of that wonderful prayer life that You give to those who expect their training for the ministry of intercession to come from not only words and thoughts, but from the Spirit of Your own life. And teach us how, in fasting and prayer, we can mature in the faith for which nothing will be impossible. Amen.

Notes for Lesson Twelve

[1] Matthew 17:19-21
[2] Matthew 17:16
[3] Matthew 10:1, Mark 6:7, Luke 9:1
[4] Mark 6:13
[5] Luke 10:17
[6] 2 Thessalonica 1:3
[7] Matthew 9:29
[8] Colossians 3:4
[9] 1 Corinthians 10:31
[10] Hebrews 12:2

Personal Notes

_____

_____

_____

_____

_____

_____

_____

LESSON 13

PRAYER AND LOVE

"And when you stand praying, if you hold anything against anyone, forgive him, so that your Father in heaven may forgive you your sins. "[1]

These words immediately follow the great prayer promise, "All things whatsoever you pray and ask for, believe that you have received them and you shall have them."[2] We have already seen how the words that preceded that promise, "Have faith in God," taught us that in prayer everything depends on the clarity of our relationship with God.

These words that follow it remind us that our relationships with others must be clear, too. Love of God and love of our neighbor are inseparable. The prayer from a heart that is not right with God or with others will not succeed.

FAITH AND LOVE ESSENTIAL TO EACH OTHER

Faith and love are essential to each other. This is a thought to which our Lord frequently gave expression. In the Sermon on the Mount, when speaking of the sixth commandment, He taught His disciples that acceptable worship of the Father was impossible if everything were not right with one's brother or sister: "Therefore, if you are offering your gift at the altar and there remember that your brother has something against you, leave your gift there in front of the altar. First go and be reconciled to your brother; then come and offer your gift."[3]

After having taught us to pray, "Forgive us our debts, as we also have forgiven our debtors," Jesus added, "But if you do not forgive men their sins, your Father will not forgive your sins."[4]

At the close of the parable of the unmerciful servant, He applies His teaching in the words, "This is how my heavenly Father will treat each of you unless you forgive your brother from your heart."[5]

Now here in Mark 11, beside the dried-up fig tree, as Jesus speaks of the power and the prayer of faith, He abruptly introduces the thought, " And when you stand praying, if you hold anything against anyone, forgive him, so that your Father in heaven may forgive you your sins."[6]

Perhaps the Lord had learned during His life that disobedience to the law of love for others was the great sin of even praying people, and the great cause of the ineffectiveness of their prayer. It is as if He wanted to lead us into His own blessed experience that nothing strengthens faith as much as the consciousness that we have given ourselves in love and compassion for those whom God loves.

FIRST LESSON—HAVE A FORGIVING DISPOSITION

The first lesson we are taught here is to have a forgiving disposition. We should pray, "Forgive us just as we have forgiven others." Scripture says "And be kind to one another, tenderhearted, forgiving one another, just as God in Christ forgave you."[7]

God's full and free forgiveness should be the model of our forgiveness of others. Otherwise our reluctant, halfhearted, forgiveness, which is not forgiveness at all, will be God's rule with us. All our prayers depend on our faith in God's pardoning grace. If God dealt with us while keeping our sins in mind, not one prayer would be heard. Pardon opens the door to all God's love and blessing. Because God has pardoned all our sins, our prayers can go through to obtain all We need.

SURE GROUND TO ANSWERED PRAYER

The deep sure ground of answer to prayer is God's forgiving love. When it has taken possession of our hearts, we pray in faith. But also, when it has taken possession of our hearts, we live in love.

God's forgiving nature, revealed to us in His love, becomes our nature. With the power of His forgiving love dwelling in us, we forgive just as He forgives.

ASSUME A GODLIKE DISPOSITION

If great injury or injustice occurs, try first of all to assume a Godlike disposition. Avoid the sense of wounded honor, the desire to maintain your rights, and the need to punish the offender. In the little annoyances of daily life, never excuse your hasty temper, sharp word, or quick judgment with the thought that you mean no harm, or that it is too much to expect your feeble human nature to really forgive the way God and Christ do. Take the command literally: *"as Christ forgave you, so you also must do."*[8]

The blood cleanses selfishness from the conscience.[9] The love it reveals is a pardoning love that takes possession of us and flows through us to others. Our forgiving love toward men is the evidence of God's forgiving love in us.[10] It is a necessary condition of the prayer of faith.

SECOND LESSON—OUR DAILY LIFE IS THE TEST OF OUR PRAYERS

The second, more general lesson, is this: *our daily life in the world is the test of our communication with God in prayer.* How often when Christians pray they do their utmost to cultivate certain frames of mind that they think will be pleasing to God. They don't understand (or they forget) that life does not consist of a lot of loose pieces that can be picked up at random and then be discarded. Life is a whole. The hour of prayer is only a small part of daily life. God's opinion of what I really am and desire is not based on the feeling I conjure up, but on the tone of my life during the day.

My relationship with God is part of my relationships with people. Failure in one will cause failure in the other. It is not necessary that it be a distinct consciousness of something wrong between my neighbor and myself. An ordinary current of thinking and judging—the unloving thoughts and words I allow to pass unnoticed—can hinder my prayer. The effective prayer of faith comes from a life given up to the will and the love of God. My prayer is not answered by God as a result of what I try to be when praying, but because of what I am when I'm not praying.

THIRD LESSON—IN LIFE EVERYTHING DEPENDS ON LOVE

All these thoughts can be gathered into a third lesson: *In life among human beings, the one thing on which everything depends is love* [seen Endnote[11]]. The spirit of forgiveness is the spirit of love. Because God is love,[12] He forgives. It is only when we are dwelling in love that we can forgive as God forgives. In love for others we have the evidence of love for the Father, the basis for our confidence before God, and the assurance that our prayer will be heard. "Let us not love in word or in tongue, but in deed and in truth. . . . by this we . . . shall assure our hearts before Him. . . . if our heart does not condemn us, we have confidence toward God. . . . And whatever we ask we receive from Him."[13]

Neither faith nor work will profit if we don't have love. Love unites us with God—it proves the reality of faith. "Have faith in God" and "love your neighbor" are both essential commandments. The right relationships with the living God above me and the living people around me are the conditions for effective prayer.

SPECIAL CONSEQUENCE OF LOVE

This love is of special consequence when we are praying for others. We sometimes commit ourselves to work for Christ out of zeal for His cause or for our own spiritual health, without giving ourselves in personal self-sacrificing love for those whose souls we seek. No wonder our faith is powerless and without victory.

View each lost sinner, however unlovable, in the light of the tender love of Jesus the shepherd searching for the lost. Look for Jesus Christ in others and take them into a heart that really loves for Jesus' sake. This is the secret of believing prayer and successful effort. Jesus speaks of love as the root of forgiveness. It is also the root of believing prayer.

BELIEVING PRAYER HEART-SEARCHING

There is nothing as heart-searching as believing prayer, or even the honest effort to pray in faith. Don't deflect that self-examination by the thought that God does not hear your prayer. "When you ask, you do not receive, because you ask with wrong motives."[14] Let that Word of God search us. Ask whether our prayer is indeed the expression of a life completely given over to the will of God and the love of people. Love is the only soil in which faith can take root and thrive. Only in the love of fixed purpose and sincere obedience can faith obtain the blessing.

Whoever gives themselves to let the love of God dwell in them, whoever in daily life loves as God loves, will have the power to believe in the love that hears every prayer. That almighty love is *the Lamb* who is in the midst of the throne.[15] It is suffering and enduring love that exists with God in prayer. The merciful will receive mercy,[16] the meek will inherit the earth.[17]

LORD, TEACH US TO PRAY

Blessed Father! You are love, and only the one who dwells in love can come into fellowship with You. Your blessed Son has taught me again how deeply true this is.

O my God! Let the Holy Spirit flood my heart with Your love. Be a fountain of love inside me that flows out to everyone around me. Let the power of believing prayer spring out of this life of love.

O my Father! Grant by the Holy Spirit that this love may be the gate through which I find life in Your love. Let the joy with which I daily forgive whomever might offend me be the proof that Your forgiveness is my power and life.

Lord Jesus! Blessed Teacher. Teach me how to forgive and to love. Let the power of Your blood make the pardon of my sins a reality, so that Your forgiveness of me and my forgiveness of others may be the very joy of heaven. Point out the weaknesses in my relationships with others that might hinder my fellowship with God. May my daily life at home and in society be the school in which strength and confidence are gathered for the prayer of faith. Amen.

NOTES FOR LESSON THIRTEEN

[1] Mark 11:25
[2] Mark 11:24 — See Lesson 10.
[3] Matthew 5:23-24
[4] Matthew 6:15
[5] Matthew 18:35
[6] Mark 11:25
[7] Ephesians 4:32
[8] Colossians 3:13
[9] Hebrews 9:14, 10:22
[10] Romans 5:5
[11] For a detailed study on God's type of love as detailed by the apostle Paul in 1 Corinthians 13, see *The Greatest Thing in the World . . . LOVE* by Henry Drummond, rewritten and expanded by Harold J. Chadwick, copyright © 1999 by Bridge-Logos Publishers, North Brunswick, NJ.
[12] 1 John 4:8, 16
[13] 1 John 3:18-19, 21-22
[14] James 4:3
[15] Revelation 5:6
[16] Matthew 5:7
[17] Matthew 5:5

PERSONAL NOTES

LESSON 14

THE POWER OF UNITED PRAYER

*"Again, I tell you that if two of you on earth
agree about anything you ask for, it will be
done for you by My Father in heaven.
For where two or three come together in
My name, there am I with them."*[1]

One of the first lessons of our Lord in His school
of prayer was not to pray visibly. Go into your closet
and be alone with the Father. When He has taught us
that the meaning of prayer is personal, individual,
contact with God, He gives us a second lesson: *we also
need public, united, prayer.* He gives us a very special
promise for the united prayer of two or three who agree
in what they ask. As a tree has its root hidden in the
ground and its stem growing up into the sunlight, so
prayer needs secrecy in which the soul meets God alone,
and it needs public fellowship with those who find their
common meeting place in the name of Jesus Christ.

REASON FOR UNITED PRAYER

The reason why there must be united prayer is plain. The bond that unites us with others is no less real and close than that which unites us to God—*He is one with them.* Grace renews not only our relationship with God, but our relationships with our fellow human beings, too. It is not only *"My* Father" that we learn to say. It would be unnatural for the children of a family to always meet their father separately, never expressing their desires or their love jointly.

Believers are not only members of one family, but of one body. Just as each member of the body depends on the other, the extent to which the Spirit can dwell in the body depends on the union and cooperation of everyone. Christians cannot reach the full blessing God is ready to bestow through His Spirit until they seek and receive it in fellowship with each other. It was to the hundred and twenty praying together in total agreement under the same roof that the Spirit came from the throne of the glorified Lord.[2] In the same way, it is in the union and fellowship of believers that the Spirit can manifest His full power.

Three elements of true, united, prayer are given to us in these words of our Lord: "Again, I tell you that if two of you on earth agree [see Endnote[3]] about anything you ask for, it will be done for you by My Father in heaven. For where two or three come together in My name, there am I with them."

FIRST ELEMENT OF UNITED PRAYER— AGREEMENT

The first is *agreement* as to the thing asked. It is not enough to generally consent to agree with anything another may ask. The object prayed for must be some special thing, a matter of distinct, united, desire. The agreement must be, as in all prayer, in spirit and in truth.

In such agreement, exactly what we are asking for becomes very clear. We find out whether we can confidently ask for it according to God's will, and whether we are ready to believe that we have received it.

SECOND ELEMENT OF UNITED PRAYER— NAME OF JESUS CHRIST

The second element is the gathering in the name of Jesus Christ. Later, we will learn much more about the necessity and the power of the name of Jesus in prayer. Here our Lord teaches us that His name must be the center and the bond of the union that makes the praying disciples one, just as a home contains and unites all who are in it. "The name of the LORD is a strong tower; the righteous run to it and are safe."[4]

That name is such a reality to those who understand and believe in it, that to meet within it is to have Him present. Jesus is powerfully attracted by the love and unity of His disciples: "where two or three *come together in my name, there am I with them.*"[5] The presence of Jesus, alive in the fellowship of His loving, praying, disciples gives united prayer its power.

THIRD ELEMENT OF UNITED PRAYER—THE CERTAIN ANSWER

The third element is the certain answer: " it will be done for you by my Father in heaven." Although a prayer meeting for maintaining religious fellowship, or for our own edification, may have its use, this was not the Savior's reason for recommending it. He meant it as a means of securing *special answer to prayer.* A prayer meeting without recognized answer to prayer should be the exception to the rule.

When we feel too weak to exercise the faith necessary to attain a distinct desire, we should seek strength in the help of others. In the unity of faith, love, and the Spirit, the power of the name and the presence of Christ acts more freely, and the answer comes more surely. The evidence that there has been true, united, prayer is the fruit—the answer, the receiving of the thing for which we have asked. "I tell you . . . *it will be done* for you by my Father in heaven."

What an extraordinary privilege united prayer is.
What a potential power it has.
Who can say what blessing might be gained . . .

- If a believing husband and wife knew they were joined together in the name of Jesus to experience His presence and power in united prayer
- If friends were aware of the mighty help two or three praying in harmony could give each other
- If in every prayer meeting the coming together in His name, in faith in His presence,

and the expectation of the answer were the prominent elements

- If in every church, united, effective, prayer was regarded as one of the chief purposes for which they are banded together
- If in the universal Church the coming of the kingdom and of the King Himself were really a matter of unceasing, united, crying to God

APOSTLE PAUL URGES UNITED PRAYER FOR HIM

To the Romans Paul writes, " I urge you, brothers, by our Lord Jesus Christ and by the love of the Spirit, to join me in my struggle by praying to God for me."[6] In answer to the prayer he expects to be delivered from his enemies and to prosper in his work.

To the Corinthians Paul declares, "On Him [God] we have set our hope that He will continue to deliver us, as you help us by your prayers. Then many will give thanks on our behalf for the gracious favor granted us in answer to the prayers of many."[7] He expects their prayer to have a real share in his deliverance.

To the Ephesians Paul writes, " And pray in the Spirit on all occasions with all kinds of prayers and requests. With this in mind, be alert and always keep on praying for all the saints. Pray also for me, that whenever I open my mouth, words may be given me"[8] He makes the welfare of other saints and the power and success in his ministry dependent on their prayers.

With the Philippians he expects that his trials will become his salvation and increase the progress of the gospel, *"through your prayers* and the help given by the Spirit of Jesus Christ."[9]

When telling the Colossians to continue praying constantly, he adds, "And pray for us, too, that God may open a door for our message."[10]

To the Thessalonians he writes, "pray for us that the message of the Lord may spread rapidly and be honored, just as it was with you."[11]

It is quite evident that Paul perceived himself as the member of a body whose sympathy and cooperation he depended on. He counted on the prayers of these churches to gain for him what otherwise might not be given. The prayers of the Church were to him as real a factor in the work of the kingdom as the power of God.

WHAT POWER COULD A CHURCH DEVELOP AND EXERCISE?

Who can say what power a church could develop and exercise if it would assume the work of praying day and night for the coming of the kingdom, for God's power, or for the salvation of souls?

Most churches think their members are to gather simply to take care of and edify each other. They don't know that God rules the world by the prayers of His saints, that prayer is the power by which Satan is conquered, and that through prayer the Church on earth has access to the powers of the heavenly world. They do not remember that Jesus has, by His promise, made every assembly in His name a gate to heaven, where His presence is to be felt, and His power experienced by the Father fulfilling their desires.

United Prayer Week

We cannot sufficiently thank God for the blessed week of united prayer, with which Christendom, in our days (1885), opens every year [see Endnote[12]]. It is of unspeakable value as proof of our unity and our faith in the power of united prayer, as a training school for the enlargement of our hearts to take in all the needs of the Church, and as a help to united persevering prayer. But it has been a special blessing as a stimulus to continued union in prayer in the smaller circles.

When God's people realize what it means to meet as one in the name of Jesus Christ, with His presence in the midst of a body united in the Holy Spirit, they will boldly claim the promise that the Father *will* do what they agree to request.

Lord, Teach Us to Pray

Blessed Lord! You ask so earnestly for the unity of Your people. Teach us how to encourage our unity with Your precious promise concerning united prayer. Show us how to join together in love and desire, so that Your presence is in our faith in the Father's answer.

O Father! We pray for those smaller circles of people who meet together so that they may become one. Remove all selfishness and self-interest, all narrowness of heart and estrangement that hinders their unity. Cast out the spirit of the world and the flesh through which Your promise loses all its power. Let the thought of Your presence in Christ and Your favor draw us all nearer to each other.

121

Grant especially, blessed Lord Jesus, that your Church may believe that it is by the power of united prayer that it can bind and loose on earth, cast out Satan, save souls, remove mountains, and hasten the coming of the kingdom.

Grant also, Lord, that my personal prayer circle and the prayer circle of my church may indeed pray with the power through which Your name and Word are glorified. Amen.

NOTES ON LESSON FOURTEEN

[1] Matthew 18:19-20

[2] Acts 1:15, 2:1

[3] *Agree* is from the Greek word, *sumphoneo.* It's the word from which we get our English word, *symphony.* It means to harmonize together in all areas so that there is not the slightest discord of any kind— just as all members of a symphony orchestra must do.

[4] Proverbs 18:10

[5] Matthew 18:20

[6] Romans 15:30

[7] 2 Corinthians 1:10-11

[8] Ephesians 6:18-19

[9] Philippians 1:19

[10] Colossians 4:3

[11] 2 Thessalonians 3:1-2

[12] The "blessed week of united prayer" referred to in the text, that "opens every year," is no longer held in Christianity, although there is in the United States a National Prayer Week each year, and individual churches throughout the world often have a week or more of prayer sometime during the year. But the prayer unity that the author speaks of as existing in Christendom in his day (1885) is no longer present in our day.

Lesson 15

The Power of Persevering Prayer

*Then He spoke a parable to them, that men
always ought to pray and not lose heart,
saying: "There was in a certain city a judge
who did not fear God nor regard man. "Now
there was a widow in that city; and she came
to him, saying, 'Get justice for me from my
adversary.' "And he would not for a while;
but afterward he said within himself, 'Though
I do not fear God nor regard man, 'yet
because this widow troubles me I will avenge
her, lest by her continual coming she weary
me.'" Then the Lord said, "Hear what the
unjust judge said. "And shall God not avenge
His own elect who cry out day and night to
Him, though He bears long with them? "I tell
you that He will avenge them speedily.
Nevertheless, when the Son of Man comes,
will He really find faith on the earth?"*[1]

Of all the mysteries of the prayer world, the need for persevering prayer is one of the greatest. We cannot easily understand why the Lord, who is so loving and longing to bless us, should have to be petitioned time after time, sometimes year after year, before the answer comes.

It is also one of the greatest practical difficulties in the exercise of believing prayer. When our repeated prayers remain unanswered, it is easy for our lazy flesh—maintaining the appearance of pious submission—to think that we must stop praying because God may have a secret reason for withholding His answer to our request.

FAITH OVERCOMES DIFFICULT OF BELIEVING PRAYER

Faith alone can overcome such difficulty. Once faith has taken its stand on God's Word and the name of Jesus, and has yielded itself to the leading of the Spirit to seek only God's will and honor in its prayer, it need not be discouraged by delay. It knows from Scripture that the power of believing prayer is considerable—real faith can never be disappointed. It knows that to exercise its power, it must be gathered up like water until the stream can come down in full force.

Prayer must often be heaped up until God sees that its measure is full. Then the answer comes. Just as each of ten thousand seeds is a part of the final harvest, frequently repeated, persevering prayer is necessary to acquire a desired blessing.

Every single believing prayer has its influence. It is stored up toward an answer that comes in due time to whomever perseveres to the end. Human thoughts and possibilities have nothing to do with it; only the Word of the living God matters. Abraham for so long "against all hope, . . . in hope believed,"[2] and then "through faith *and patience* inherit[ed] the promise."[3] Wait and pray often for the coming of the Lord to fulfill His promise.

WHEN THE ANSWER DOES NOT COME IMMEDIATELY

When the answer to our prayer does not come at once, we should combine quiet patience and joyful confidence in our persevering prayer. To enable us to do this, we must try to understand two words in which our Lord describes the character and conduct of our God and Father toward those who cry day and night to Him: "though He *bears long* [see Endnote[4]] with them? I tell you that He will avenge them *speedily*."[5]

The Master uses the word *speedily*. The blessing is all prepared. The Father is not only willing, but is most anxious to give them what they ask. His everlasting love burns with His longing desire to reveal itself fully to His beloved and to satisfy their needs. God will not delay one moment longer than is absolutely necessary. He will do everything in His power to hasten the answer.

But why—if this is true and God's power is infinite—does it often take so long to get an answer to prayer? And why must God's own elect so often, in

125

the midst of suffering and conflict, cry day and night? "through He *bears long* [waits patiently] with them." "See how the farmer waits for the precious fruit of the earth, *waiting patiently* for it until it receives the early and latter rain."[6]

Of course the farmer longs for the harvest. But the crop must have its full term of sunshine and rain, so it requires plenty of patience. A child so often wants to pick the half-ripe fruit, while the farmer knows to wait until the proper time.

LAW OF GRADUAL GROWTH

In our spiritual nature, we, too, are under the law of gradual growth that reigns in all created life. Only on the path of development can we reach our divine destiny. And only the Father, who determines the times and seasons, knows the moment when the soul or the Church is ripened to that fullness of faith in which it can really take and keep a blessing.

As a mother who longs to have her only child home from school, and yet waits patiently until the time of training that day is completed, so it is with God and His children.

SECRETS OF PERSEVERANCE

Insight into this truth should lead us to cultivate the corresponding attitudes of *patience, faith, waiting,* and *praise,* which are the secret of perseverance. By faith in the promise of God, we know that we *have* the petitions we have asked of Him.[7] Faith holds the answer in the promise as an unseen spiritual possession.[8] It rejoices in it and praises God for it.

But there is a difference between this kind of faith and the clearer, fuller, riper faith that obtains the promise as a present experience. It is in persevering, confident, and praising prayer that the soul grows up into full union with its Lord in which it can possess the blessing in Him.

There may be things around us that have to be corrected through prayer before the answer can fully happen. The faith that has, according to the command, believed that it has received,[9] can allow God to take His time. It knows it has and must succeed. In quiet, persistent, and determined perseverance it continues in prayer and thanksgiving until the blessing comes.

So we see a combination of what at first sight appears to be so contradictory—the faith that rejoices in God's answer as a present possession, combined with the patience that cries day and night until that answer comes. The waiting child meets God triumphantly with patient faith.

(The great danger in this school is the temptation to think that it may not be God's will to give us what we desire. If our prayer agrees with God's Word and is led by the Spirit, don't give way to these fears.)

LEARN TO GIVE GOD TIME

God needs time with us. In daily fellowship with Him, we must give Him time to exercise the full influence of His presence in us. Day by day, as we are kept waiting, it is necessary that faith be given time to prove its reality and fill our beings entirely. God will lead us from faith to vision, and we will see His glory.

Don't let delay shake your faith, for it is faith that will provide the answer in time. *Each believing prayer is a step nearer to the final victory.* It ripens the fruit, conquers hindrances in the unseen world, and hastens the end.

Learn to give your Father time. He is patiently watching over you. He wants your blessing to be rich, full, and sure. Give Him time, but continue praying day and night. And above all, remember the promise: "I tell you that He will avenge them *speedily.*"

BLESSING OF PERSEVERING PRAYER

The blessing of such persevering prayer is indescribable. There is nothing that examines the heart more closely than the prayer of faith. It teaches you to discover, confess, and give up everything that hinders the coming of the blessing—everything that is not in accordance with the Father's will. It leads to closer fellowship with Him who alone can teach you to pray. Complete surrender becomes possible under the covering of the blood and the Spirit. Give God time. He will perfect whatever concerns you.

MAINTAIN THE SAME PRAYER ATTITUDE

Let your attitude be the same whether you are praying for yourself or for others. All labor, bodily or mental, needs time and effort. We must give *ourselves up* to it. Nature reveals her secrets and yields her treasures only to diligent and thoughtful labor.

However little we can understand it, spiritual husbandry is always the same: The seed we sow in the soil of heaven, the efforts we put forth, and the influence we seek to exert in the world above all require our *complete surrender* in prayer. Maintain great confidence that when the time is right, we will reap an abundant harvest if we don't give up.[10]

Let us especially learn this lesson as we pray for the Church of Christ. She is indeed like a poor widow in the absence of her Lord, apparently at the mercy of her adversary and helpless to correct the situation. When we pray for His Church or any portion of it that is under the power of the world, let us ask Him to visit her with mighty workings in His Spirit to prepare her for His coming.

Pray in the assured faith that prayer does help. Unceasing prayer will bring the answer. Just give God time. And remember this day and night: "Hear what the unjust judge said. And shall God not avenge His own elect who cry out day and night to Him, though He *bears long* with them? I tell you that *He will avenge them speedily.*"

LORD, TEACH US HOW TO PRAY

O Lord my God! Teach me how to know Your way and in faith to learn what Your beloved Son has taught: "He will avenge them speedily." Let Your tender love, and the delight You have in hearing and blessing Your children, lead me implicitly to accept the promise that we may have whatever we ask for, and that the answer will be seen in due time.

Lord! We understand nature's seasons. We know how to wait for the fruit we long for. Fill us with the assurance that You won't delay one moment longer than is necessary, and that our faith will hasten the answer.

Blessed Master! You have said that God's elect appeal to Him day and night. Please teach us to understand this. You know how quickly we become tired. Perhaps we feel that the divine majesty of the Father is so far beyond the reach of our continued prayer that it is not becoming for us to plead with Him too much.

O Lord! Teach me how real the labor of prayer is. I know that when I fail at something here on earth, I can often succeed by renewed and more continuous effort, and by taking more time and thought. Show me how, by giving myself more entirely to prayer—by actually living in prayer— I can obtain what I have asked for.

Above all, O Blessed teacher, author and perfecter of my faith, let my whole life be one of faith in the Son of God who loved me and gave Himself for me. In You my prayer gains acceptance and I have the assurance of the answer.

Lord Jesus! In such faith I will pray always, and never cease. Amen.

[Author's Note]

The need of persevering prayer appears to be at variance with the faith that knows it has received what it asks for, as noted in Mark 11:24. One of the mysteries of the Divine life is the harmony between sudden, complete, possession and slow, imperfect, appropriation. Here persevering prayer appears to be the school in which the soul is strengthened for the boldness of faith.

Considering the diversity of operations of the Spirit, there may be some in whom faith takes the form of persistent waiting. For others, triumphant thanksgiving appears the only proper expression of the assurance of having been heard.

NOTES ON LESSON FIFTEEN

[1] Luke 18:1-8, NKJV
[2] Romans 4:18
[3] Hebrews 6:12
[4] *Bears long* also has the sense of enduring or being patiently tolerant—waiting patiently.
[5] Luke 18:7-8
[6] James 5:7
[7] 1 John 5:15
[8] Hebrews 11:1
[9] Mark 11:24
[10] Galatians 6:9

PERSONAL NOTES

_____

_____

_____

_____

LESSON 16

PRAYER IN HARMONY WITH GOD

"Father, I thank you that you have heard me.
I knew that you always hear me."[1]
"You are My Son, Today I have begotten You.
Ask of Me, and I will give You."[2]

In the New Testament, we find a distinction made between *faith* and *knowledge*. "For to one is given the word of wisdom through the Spirit, to another the word of knowledge through the same Spirit, to another faith by the same Spirit"[3]

In a child or an uninformed Christian there may be much faith with little knowledge. Childlike simplicity accepts the truth without difficulty, and often cares little to give any reason for its faith but *God said it*. But it is the will of God that we should love and serve Him, not only with all the heart, but also with all the mind.[4]

God wants us to develop an insight into the divine wisdom and beauty of all His ways, words, and works.

Only in this way will the believer be able to fully approach and rightly adore the glory of God's grace. And only thus can our hearts intelligently understand the treasures of wisdom and knowledge that exist in redemption, preparing us to join in the highest note of the song that rises before the throne: "Oh, the depth of the riches both of the wisdom and knowledge of God!"[5]

DEEPEST QUESTIONS ABOUT PRAYER

While prayer and faith are so simple that the newborn convert can pray with power, more mature Christians may find in the doctrine of prayer some of their deepest questions:

- How extensive is the power of prayer?
- How can God grant to prayer such mighty power?
- How can prayer be harmonized with the will of God?
- How can God's sovereignty and our will— God's liberty and ours—be reconciled?

These and similar questions are appropriate subjects for Christian meditation and inquiry. The more earnestly and reverently we approach such mysteries, the more we will fall down in adoring wonder to praise Him who has in prayer given such power to us.

PRAYER AND THE PERFECTION OF GOD

One of the difficulties with regard to prayer is the result of the perfection of God. He is absolutely independent of everything outside of Himself. He is an infinite being who owes what He is to Himself alone. With His wise and holy will, He has determined Himself and everything that is to be. This raises additional questions:

- How can our prayer influence God?
- How can He be moved by prayer to do what He otherwise would not do?
- Isn't the promise of an answer to prayer simply a condescension to our weakness?
- Is the power of prayer anything more than an accommodation of our mode of thought, because the accomplishments of deity are never dependent on any outside action?
- Isn't the real blessing of prayer simply the influence it exerts on us?

KEY TO THE MYSTERY OF THE HOLY TRINITY

Seeking answers to such questions provides the key to the very being of God in the mystery of the Holy Trinity. If God were only one Person, shut up within Himself, there could be no thought of nearness to Him or influence on Him. But in God there are three Persons: *Father, Son* and *Holy Spirit*. It is in the Holy Spirit that the Father and Son have their living bond of unity and fellowship. When the Father gave the Son a place next to Himself as His equal and His counselor, He opened a way for prayer and its influence into the very inmost life of the Trinity itself.

On earth, just as in heaven, the whole relationship between Father and Son is that of giving and taking. If the taking is to be as voluntary and self-determined as

135

the giving, the Son must ask and receive. "You are My Son, Today I have begotten You. Ask of Me, and I will give You."[6]

The Father gave the Son the place and the power to influence Him. The Son's asking wasn't just for show. It was one of those life-movements in which the love of the Father and the Son met and completed each other. The Father had determined that He would not be alone in His counsels—*their fulfillment would depend on the Son's asking and receiving.* Thus asking was in the very being and life of God. Prayer on earth was to be the reflection and the outflow of this.

Jesus said, "I knew that you always hear me."[7] Just as the sonship of Jesus on earth cannot be separated from His sonship in heaven, His prayer on earth is the continuation and the counterpart of His asking in heaven. His prayer is the link between the eternal asking of the only begotten Son in the bosom of the Father[8] and the prayer of Christians on earth. Prayer has its rise and its deepest source in the very being of God. In the bosom of the Trinity nothing is ever done without prayer—the asking of the Son and the giving of the Father.

HOW PRAYER AFFECTS GOD

This may help us to understand how the prayer of Christians, going through the Son, can have an effect on God. God's decrees are not made without reference to the Son, His petition, or a petition sent up through Him.[9] The Lord Jesus is the first begotten, the head and heir of all things.[10]

As the representative of all creation, Christ always has a voice in the Father's decisions. In the decrees of the eternal purpose, room was always left for the liberty of the Son as mediator[11] and intercessor.[12] The same holds true for the petitions of all who draw near to the Father through the Son.

GOD NOT BOUND BY TIME

If Christ's liberty and power to influence the Father seems to be at variance with the immutability of the divine decrees, remember that God doesn't have a past, as we do, to which He is irrevocably bound. The distinctions of time have no meaning to Him who inhabits eternity.

Eternity is an ever-present *now,* in which the past never passes and the future is always present. To meet our human comprehension of time, the Scriptures must speak of past decrees and a coming future.

GOD'S UNCHANGING NATURE AND HUMAN LIBERTY IN PERFECT HARMONY

In reality, the unchanging nature of God's plan is still in perfect harmony with His liberty to do whatever He wills. The prayers of the Son and His people were not included in the eternal decrees simply for show. Rather, the Father listens with His heart to every prayer that rises through the Son. God really does allow Himself to be moved by prayer to do what He otherwise would not have done.

This perfect, harmonious, union of divine sovereignty and human liberty is an unfathomable mystery because God as *the Eternal One.* transcends all our thoughts. But let it be our comfort and strength to know that in the eternal fellowship of the Father and the Son, the power of prayer has its origin and certainty. Through our union with the Son, our prayer is taken up and can have its influence in the inner life of the Blessed Trinity. God's decrees are no iron framework against which humanity's liberty struggles vainly.

GOD IS LIVING LOVE

God Himself is living love, Who in His Son as man has entered into the tenderest relationship with all that is human. Through the Holy Spirit, He takes up everything human into the divine life of love, leaving Himself free to give every human prayer its place in His government of the world.

In the light of such thoughts, the doctrine of the blessed Trinity is no longer an abstract speculation, but the living manifestation of how we are taken up into the fellowship of God, our prayers becoming a real factor in God's rule of this earth. We can catch a glimpse of the light shining out from the eternal world in words such as these: *"through Him* we . . . have access *by one Spirit* to *the Father."*[13]

LORD, TEACH US TO PRAY

Everlasting God! In deep reverence I worship before the holy mystery of Your divine being. If it pleases You, most glorious God, to reveal some of that mystery to me, I would bow with fear and trembling rather than sin against You as I meditated on Your glory.

Father! I thank You for being not only the Father

of Your children here on earth, but the Father of Jesus Christ through eternity. Thank You for hearing our prayers and for having given Christ's asking a place in Your eternal plan. Thank You also for sending Christ to earth and for His blessed communication with You in heaven. There has always been room in Your counsel for His prayers and the answers to those prayers.

I thank You above all that through Christ's true human nature on Your throne above, and through your Holy Spirit in our human nature here below, a way has been opened by which every human cry of need can be received into Your life and love, and always obtain an answer.

Blessed Jesus! As the Son, You have opened this path of prayer and assured us of an answer. We beseech You to teach us how to pray. Let our prayers be the sign that we are true children of God, so that we, like You, know that the Father always hears us. Amen.

Notes on Lesson Sixteen

[1] John 11:41.42
[2] Psalm 2:7-8
[3] 1 Corinthians 12:8-9
[4] Matthew 22:37, Mark 12:30, Luke 10:27
[5] Romans 11:33 — There is no scriptural indication that these words of Paul are sung before the throne of God. The author may have had in mind the songs sung in chapters 4 and 5 of the Book of Revelation.
[6] Psalm 2:7-8

[7] John 11:42
[8] John 1:18
[9] Ephesians 2:18
[10] Hebrews 1:2
[11] 1 Timothy 2:5
[12] Hebrews 7:25
[13] Ephesians 2:18

PERSONAL NOTES

_____

_____

_____

_____

_____

_____

_____

_____

LESSON 17

PRAYER IN HARMONY WITH THE DESTINY OF HUMANITY

And He said to them, "Whose image and
inscription is this?"[1]
"Let Us make man in Our image,
according to Our likeness."[2]

"Whose image . . . is this?" It was with this question that Jesus foiled His enemies when they tried to trick Him, settling the matter of responsibility in regard to paying taxes. The question and the principle it involves are universally applicable, particularly to humanity itself. Bearing God's image decides humanity's destiny. We belong to God and prayer to God is what we were created for. Prayer is part of the wondrous likeness we bear to His divine original. It is the earthly likeness of the deep mystery of the fellowship of love in which the Trinity has its blessedness.

The more we meditate on what prayer is and on the wonderful power it has with God, the more we have to ask how we are so special that such a place in God's plan has been allotted to us. Sin has so degraded humankind that we can't conceive of what we were meant to be based on what we are now. We must turn back to God's own record of our creation to find what God's purpose was, and what capacities we were given to fulfill that purpose.

OUR DESTINY

Our destiny appears clearly in God's language at creation. It was *to fill*, to *subdue,* and to *have dominion* over the earth and everything in it.[3] These three expressions show us that we were intended, as God's representative, to rule here on earth.

As God's deputy, we were to fill God's place, keeping everything in subjection to Him. It was the will of God that everything done on earth should be done through us—i.e., the development of the earth was to be entirely in our hands.

POSITION AND POWER IN ACCORDANCE WITH DESTINY

The position we were to occupy and the power at our disposal was in accordance with that destiny. When an earthly sovereign sends a representative to a distant province, that representative advises the sovereign as to the policy to be adopted there. The sovereign follows that advice, doing whatever is necessary to enact the policy and maintain the dignity of his empire. If the sovereign, however, doesn't approve of the policy, the representative is replaced with someone who better understands the sovereign's desires for the empire. But as long as the representative is trusted, the instituted policy is carried out.

As God's representative, we were to have ruled. Everything was to have been done according to humankind's will. In our advice and at our request, heaven was to have bestowed its blessing on earth. Our prayers were to have been the natural channels through which the Lord in heaven and we, as lords of this world, communicated. The destinies of the world were given into the power of our wishes, our wills, and our prayers.

But with the advent of sin, all this underwent a terrible change. Humankind's fall brought all creation under the curse. God's planned redemption, however, brought the beginning of a glorious restoration.

ABRAHAM'S PRAYERS

In Abraham, God began to make Himself a people from whom kings (not to mention the great King) would emerge. We see how Abraham's prayer power affected the destinies of those who came into contact with him. In Abraham we see how prayer is not just the means of obtaining blessing for ourselves, it is the exercise of a royal prerogative to influence the destinies of people and the will of God that rules them.

We do not once find Abraham praying for himself. His prayers for Sodom and Lot, for Abimelech, and for Ishmael prove that those who are God's friends have the power to control the history of those around them.

ALWAYS OUR DESTINY

This has been humankind's destiny from the first. But the Scriptures tells us more: God could entrust us with such a high calling because He created us in His *own image and likeness.* The external responsibility was not committed to us without the inner fitness. The root of our inner resemblance to God is in our nature to have dominion, to be rulers of all. There is an inner agreement and harmony between God and us, an embryonic God-likeness, which gives us a real fitness for being mediators between God and His world.

We—humankind, humanity—were to be prophets, priests, and kings, to interpret God's will, to represent nature's needs, to receive and dispense God's bounty. It was in bearing God's image that we could bear God's rule. We were created so much like God—so capable of entering into God's purposes and carrying out His plans—that God could trust us with the wonderful privilege of asking for and obtaining what the world might need.

SIN DESTROYS, GRACE RESTORES

Although sin has for a time frustrated God's plans, prayer still remains what it would have been if humanity had never fallen—the proof of our God-likeness, the vehicle of our communication with the Father, and the power that is allowed to hold the hand that holds the destinies of the universe.

We are of divine origin, created for and capable of possessing king-like liberty. Our prayers are not merely cries for mercy, they are the greatest execution of our wills.

What sin destroyed, grace has restored. What the first Adam lost, the last Adam won back.[4] In Christ, we regain our original position, and the Church, abiding in Christ, inherits the promise, "ask what you desire, and it shall be done for you."[5]

THE PROMISE IS FOR THE POSITION

To begin with, such a promise does by no means refer to the grace or blessing we need for ourselves. It has reference to our position as the fruit-bearing branches of the heavenly Vine,[6] who, like Him, only live for the work and glory of the Father.[7] It is for those who abide in Him, who have forsaken themselves for a life of obedience and self-sacrifice in Him, who have completely surrendered to the interests of the Father and His kingdom. They understand how their redemption through Christ has brought them back to their original destiny, restoring God's image and the power to have dominion.

Such people indeed have the power—each in their own area—to obtain and dispense the powers of heaven here on earth. With holy boldness they may make known what they will. They live as priests in God's presence. They are kings possessing the powers of the world to come [see Endnote[8]]. They enter upon the fulfillment of the promise, ""ask what you desire, and it shall be done for you."

HIGH AND HOLY CALLING

Your calling is higher and holier than you know. God wants to rule the world through your members. He wants you to be His kings and priests. Your prayers can bestow and withhold the blessings of heaven.

In His elect who are not content just to be saved, but who surrender themselves completely, the Father will fulfill all His glorious counsel through them just as He does through the Son. In His elect, who cry day and night to Him, God wants to prove how wonderful humanity's original destiny was.

Adam and Eve were the image-bearers of God on earth, which was indeed given to them to rule.[9] When they fell, everything fell with them. Now the whole creation groans and travails in pain together.[10]

GOD'S REDEEMED PEOPLE

But now we have been redeemed, and the restoration of the original dignity has begun. It is God's purpose that the fulfillment of His eternal purpose and the coming of His kingdom should depend on His people. They abide in Christ and are ready to accept Him as their head, their great Priest-King. In their prayers they boldly say what they desire God to do for them.

As God's image-bearer and representatives on earth, the redeemed of the Lord have the power to determine the history of this earth through their prayers. Humankind was created and then redeemed to pray, and by its prayer to have dominion.

LORD, TEACH US TO PRAY

Lord! What are human beings that you are mindful of them, mortals that you care for them?

Yet you have made them a little lower than God, and crowned them with glory and honor.

You have given them dominion over the works of your hands; you have put all things under their feet.[11]

O LORD, our Sovereign, how majestic is your name in all the earth![12]

****

Lord God! Human beings have sunk so low because of sin. And how terribly it has darkened their minds. They don't even know their divine destiny is to be Your servants and representatives. How sad it is that even when their eyes are opened people are so unready to accept their calling. They could have such power with You and with people.

Lord Jesus! Through You, the Father has again crowned us with glory and honor—opening the way for us to be what He wants us to be.

O Lord! Have mercy on Your people—Your heritage. Work mightily with us in Your Church. Teach Your believing disciples to accept and to go forth in their royal priesthood. Teach us to use the power of prayer to which You have given such wonderful promises, to serve Your kingdom, to rule over the nations, and to make the name of God glorious on the earth.[13] Amen.

NOTES ON LESSON SEVENTEEN

[1] Matthew 22:20
[2] Genesis 1:26, NRSV
[3] Genesis 1:28

[4] 1 Corinthians 15:45
[5] John 15:7
[6] John 15:1-5
[7] John 14:13, 15:8
[8] "God is seeking priests from among His created beings. A human priesthood is one of the essential parts of His eternal plan. *To rule* creation by humanity is His design.

"Priesthood is the appointed link between heaven and earth, the channel of communication between the sinner and God. Such a priesthood, insofar as expiation is concerned, is in the hands of the Son of God alone; insofar as it is to be the medium of communication between Creator and creature, is also in the hands of the redeemed people of the Church of God.

"God is seeking kings. Not out of the ranks of angels. Fallen humanity must furnish Him with the rulers of His universe. Human hands must wield the scepter, human heads must wear the crown." *(The Rent Veil*, by Dr. H. Bonar.)
[9] Genesis 1:28
[10] Romans 8:22
[11] Psalm 8:4-6, NRSV
[12] Psalm 8:1, NRSV
[13] Psalm 72:19

PERSONAL NOTES

_____

_____

_____

LESSON 18

POWER FOR PRAYING AND WORKING

I tell you the truth, anyone who has faith
in Me will do what I have been doing. He
will do even greater things than these,
because I am going to the Father.
And I will do whatever you ask in My
name, so that the Son may bring glory to
the Father.
You may ask Me for anything in My
name, and I will do it.[1]

The Savior opened His public ministry in the Sermon on the Mount with the same subject He uses here in His parting address from the gospel of John—*prayer*. But there is a difference.

The Sermon on the Mount is directed to disciples who have just entered His school, scarcely knowing that God is their Father, whose prayers have reference chiefly to their personal needs. In this closing address, He speaks to disciples whose training time is coming to an end, who are ready as His messengers to take His place and continue His work.

Christ's first lesson had been—be childlike, pray in faith, and trust the Father to give you everything good. Here He points to something higher. The disciples are now His friends. He has told them everything He knows about the Father. They are His messengers into whose hands the care of His work and kingdom on earth is to be entrusted.

DOING GREATER WORKS THAN JESUS

Now they must assume their care of His work and kingdom, performing even greater works than Jesus in the power of His approaching exaltation. Prayer is to be the channel through which that power is received. With Christ's ascension to the Father, a new epoch for both their working and their praying commences.

This connection comes out clearly in our text-verses from John, chapter fourteen. As His body here on earth, as those who are one with Him in heaven, the disciples are now to do greater works than He had done. Their successes and their victories are to be greater than His. Jesus mentions two reasons for this:

1. He was going to the Father to receive all power

2. They could now ask for and expect that power in His name. " I am going to the Father . . . *And* (notice this *and*) I will do whatever you ask in my name

Jesus' going to the Father brings a double blessing. The disciples could ask for and receive everything in

150

His name, and so would do the greater works. This first mention of prayer in our Savior's parting words teaches us two most important lessons—(1) whoever wants to do the works of Jesus must pray in His name; (2) whoever prays in His name must work in His name.

LESSON ONE: PRAY IN HIS NAME

In prayer the power for work is obtained. When Jesus was here on earth, He did the greatest works himself. Demons that the disciples could not cast out fled at His word. When He went to be with the Father, He was no longer here in a body to work directly. The disciples were now His body. All His work from the throne in heaven must and could be done here on earth through them.

Now that Christ was leaving the scene and could only work through commissioners, it might have been expected that the works would be fewer and weaker. He assures us of the contrary: "I tell you the truth, anyone who has faith in Me will do what I have been doing. He will do even greater things than these, because I am going to the Father."[2]

His approaching death was to be a breaking down of the power of sin. With the resurrection, the powers of the eternal life were to take possession of the human body and obtain supremacy over human life. With His ascension, Christ was to receive the power to communicate the Holy Spirit completely to His body. The union—the oneness between Him on the throne and those on earth—was to be so intensely and divinely perfect, that He meant it as the literal truth: "He will do even greater things than these, because I am going to the Father."

THE GREATER THINGS

How true it was that they would do greater things than Jesus. During three years of personal labor on earth, Jesus gathered little more than five hundred disciples, most of whom were so powerless that they were not much help to His cause.[3] Men like Peter and Paul did much greater things than He had done. From the throne He could do through them what He himself in His humiliation could not yet do. He could ask the Father, receiving and bestowing new power for the greater works.

What was true for the early disciples is true for us. As we believe and ask in His name, the power comes and takes possession of us also to do the greater works.

LITTLE POWER SEEN TODAY

Alas, today there is little or nothing to be seen of the power to do anything like Christ's works, not to mention anything greater. There can only be one reason—the belief in Him and the believing prayer in His name are absent.

Every child of God must learn this lesson—*prayer in the name of Jesus Christ is the only way to share in the mighty power that Christ has received from the Father for His people* [see Endnote[4]]. It is in this power alone that the believer can do greater works. To every complaint about difficulties or lack of success, Jesus gives this one answer: "I tell you the truth, anyone who has faith in Me will do what I have been doing. He will do even greater things than these, because I am going to the Father." and "you may ask Me for anything in My name, and I will do it."

PRAY IN HIS NAME

If you want to do the work of Jesus, believe and become linked to Him, the Almighty One, and then pray the prayer of faith in His name.

Without this our work is just human and carnal. It may have some use in restraining sin or in preparing the way for a blessing, but the real power is missing. Effective working first needs effective praying.

LESSON TWO: WHOEVER PRAYS *MUST* WORK

It is for power to work that prayer has such great promises. Power for the effective prayer of faith is gained through working. Our blessed Lord repeats no less than six times (John 14:13-14; 15:7, 16; 16:23-24) those unlimited prayer-promises that evoke anxious questions as to their real meaning: *whatever, anything, what you will, ask and you will receive.*[5]

Many believers have read these with joy and hope, and in deep earnestness of soul have attempted to plead them for their own needs, and have come away disappointed. The simple reason was that they separated the promise from its context.

FREE USE OF NAME CONNECTED TO WORKS

The Lord gave the wonderful promise of the free use of His name with the Father in conjunction with *doing His works.* The disciple who lives only for Jesus' work and kingdom, for His will and honor, will be given the power to appropriate the promise.

Those grasping the promise only when they want something special for themselves will be disappointed, because they are making Jesus the servant of their own comforts. But whoever wants to pray the effective prayer of faith because they need it for the work of the Master will learn it, because they have made themselves the servant of their Lord's interests. Prayer not only teaches and strengthens us for work, work teaches and strengthens us for prayer.

"I tell you that to everyone who has, more will be given."[6]

Whoever is "faithful with a few things; I will put . . . in charge of many things."[7]

With the small amount of grace we have already received, let us give ourselves to the Master for His work. It will be to us a real school of prayer. When Moses had to take full charge of a rebellious people, he felt the need, and also the courage, to speak boldly to God and to ask great things of Him.[8] As you give yourself entirely to God for His work, you will feel that these great promises are exactly what you need, and that you may most confidently expect nothing less.

CALLED AND APPOINTED

You are called—you are *appointed*—to do the works of Jesus, and even greater works. He went to the Father to get the power to do them in and through *you*. Remember His promise: "*I will do whatever you ask* in My name."

Give yourself to Jesus Christ and live to do His works, and you will learn how to obtain wonderful answers to prayer. You will learn to do not only what He did when He was on earth, but much more. With disciples full of faith in Him, boldly asking great things in prayer, Christ can conquer the world.

LORD, TEACH US TO PRAY

O my Lord! Once again, I am hearing You say things that are beyond my comprehension. I can do nothing but accept them and keep them in simple, childlike, faith as Your gift to me. You have said that because of Your going to be with the Father, anyone who believes in You can do not only the things You did, but greater things as well.

Lord! I worship You as the Glorified One and eagerly await the fulfillment of Your promise. May my whole life be one of continued believing in You. Purify and sanctify my heart. Make it so tenderly susceptible to You and Your love that believing in You will become its very breath.

You have said that because You went to the Father, You will do whatever we ask You to do. You want Your people to share your power. From Your throne, You want to work through them as members of your body in response to their believing prayers in Your name. You have promised us power in our prayers to You, and power in our work here on earth.

Blessed Lord! Forgive us for not believing You and Your promise more. Because of our lack of faith, we have failed to demonstrate how You are

155

faithful to fulfill that promise. Please forgive us for so little honoring Your all-prevailing name in heaven and on earth.

Lord! Teach me to pray so that I can prove Your name is all-powerful with God, with mortals, and with the Devil and his demons. Teach me to work and to pray in a way that glorifies You, and do Your great works through me. Amen.

NOTES ON LESSON EIGHTEEN

[1] John 14:12-14

[2] John 14:12

[3] And only 120 gathered together after Jesus' ascension—see Acts 1:15.

[4] Matthew 28:18—The KJV reads: "All power is given unto me in heaven and in earth." All other versions read, "All authority . . ." But divine power is inherent in divine authority.

[5] John 14:13-14; 15:7, 16; 16:23-24

[6] Luke 19:26

[7] Matthew 25:21

[8] Exodus 33:12, 15, 18

PERSONAL NOTES

_____

_____

_____

LESSON 19

THE MAIN PURPOSE OF PRAYER

"I go to My Father.
And whatever you ask in My name, that I
will do, that the Father may be glorified
in the Son."[1]

"That the Father may be glorified in the Son"—it
is to this end that Jesus on His throne in glory will do
everything we ask in His name. Every answer to prayer
He gives will have this as its object. When there is no
prospect of this object being obtained, He will not
answer the prayer. It follows as a matter of course that
with us, as with Jesus, this must be the essential element
in our petitions. The glory of the Father must be the
aim—the very soul and life—of our prayer.

This was Jesus' goal when He was on earth: "I seek
not mine own honor; I seek the honor of Him that sent
me" [see Endnote[2]].

In such works we have the keynote of Jesus' life. The first words of His high-priestly prayer voice it: "Father, . . . Glorify your Son, *that your Son also may glorify you. . . . "I have glorified You* on the earth."[3]

His reason for asking to be taken up into the glory He had with the Father is a twofold one: He has glorified Him on earth, He will still glorify Him in heaven. All He asks is to be able to glorify the Father more.

OUR PRAYERS CANNOT FAIL

As we begin to share Jesus' feeling on this point, gratifying Him by making the Father's glory our chief object in prayer, too, our prayer cannot fail to get an answer. The beloved Son has said that nothing glorifies the Father more than His doing what we ask.

Jesus, therefore, won't miss any opportunity to do what we request. Let us make His aim ours. Let the glory of the Father be the link between our asking and His doing.

JESUS' WORDS ARE A TWO-EDGED SWORD

Jesus' words come indeed as a sharp two-edged sword, dividing the soul and the spirit, and quickly discerning the thoughts and intents of the heart.[4] In His prayers on earth, His intercession in heaven, and His promise of an answer to our prayers, Jesus makes His first object the glory of His Father.

Is this our object, too? Or are self-interest and self-will the strongest motives urging us to pray? A distinct, conscious, longing for the glory of the Father must animate our prayers.

DESIRING THE GLORY OF THE FATHER

As believers we do at times desire the glory of the Father, but don't desire it enough. The reason for this failure is that the separation between the spirit of our daily life and the spirit at our hour of prayer is too wide. Desire for the glory of the Father is not something we can arouse and present to our Lord when we prepare ourselves to pray. Only when the whole life in all its parts are given up to God's glory can we really pray to Christ's glory, too.

"Do all to the glory of God,"[5] and "Ask all to the glory of God."[6] These twin commands are inseparable. Obedience to the former is the secret of grace for the latter. Living for the glory of God is the condition of the prayers that Jesus can answer.

PRAYING FOR GLORY OF GOD
RIGHT AND NATURAL

This demand that prayer be to the glory of God is quite right and natural. Only the Lord is glorious. There is no glory but His, and what He allots to His creations. Creation exists to show forth His glory. Everything that doesn't glorify Him is sinful, dark, and dead. It is only in the glorifying of God that creatures can find glory. What the Son of Man did—giving Himself wholly to glorify the Father[7] —is nothing but the simple duty of every redeemed one, who will also receive Christ's reward.

We cannot attain a life with God's glory as our only aim by any effort of our own. It is only in Christ

Jesus that such a life can be found. Yes, blessed be God! His life is our life. He gave *himself for* us.

Christ is now our life. It is essential, to discover, confess, and deny *self* because it takes God's place. Only the presence and rule of Christ in our hearts[8] can cast out all self-glorification, replacing it with His own God-glorifying life and Spirit. It is Christ Jesus, who longs to glorify the Father in hearing our prayers, who will teach us to live and to pray to the glory of God.

SEEING THE WORTHINESS OF GOD

Nothing but seeing the worthiness of God has the power to urge our slothful hearts to yield themselves to our Lord to work this in us. There is nothing more needed than a glimpse of how worthy of glory the Father is. Our faith should learn to bow before Him in adoring worship, ascribing to Him alone the kingdom, the power, and the glory,[9] and yielding ourselves to life in His light. Surely we will be stirred to say, "To Him alone be glory."

We will then look to our Lord Jesus with new intensity of desire for a life that refuses to recognize anything but the glory of God. When there are not enough prayers to be answered, the Father is not glorified.[10] It is our duty to live and pray so that our prayers can be answered. For the sake of God's glory, let us learn to pray well.

What a humbling thought it is, that so often there is earnest prayer in which the desire for our own joy or pleasure is far stronger than any desire for God's glory. No wonder there are so many unanswered prayers. Here we have the secret—*God cannot be glorified when that glory is not the object of our prayers.* Those who want to pray the prayer of faith must give themselves to live literally so that the Father in all things is glorified in them. This must be their aim—without it there cannot be a prayer of faith.

SEEKING SELF-GLORY

"How can you believe," said Jesus, "when you accept glory from one another and do not seek the glory that comes from the one who alone is God?"[11] When we seek our own glory among people, we make faith impossible. Only the deep, intense, self-sacrifice that gives up its own glory and seeks the glory of God wakens in the soul that spiritual susceptibility to divine faith . The surrender to God and the expectation that He will show His glory in hearing us are essential. Only those who seek God's glory will see it in the answers to their prayers.

How do we accomplish this? Let us begin with a confession. The glory of God hasn't really been an all absorbing passion in our lives and our prayers. We have seldom lived in the likeness of the Son and in sympathy with Him for God and His glory alone. Take time to allow the Holy Spirit to reveal how deficient we have been in this. True knowledge and confession of sin are the sure path to deliverance.

LOOKING TO JESUS CHRIST

Let us then look to Jesus Christ.[12] In death He glorified God—through death He was glorified with Him. It is by dying—being dead to self and living for God—that we can glorify Him. This death to self, this life to the glory of God, is what Christ gives and lives in each one who can trust Him for it. Let the spirit of our daily lives consist of the decision to live only for the glory of the Father as Jesus did, the acceptance of Christ with His life and strength working it in us, and the joyful assurance that we can live for the glory of God because Christ lives in us and helps us to live this way.

The Holy Spirit is waiting to make it our experience, if we will only trust and let Him. Don't hold back through unbelief. Confidently do everything for the glory of God. Our obedience will please the Father. The Holy Spirit will seal us[13] within with the consciousness that we are living for God and His glory.

HARMONY WITH CHRIST

What quiet peace and power will be in our prayers when we know that we are in perfect harmony with Christ, who promises to do what we ask, "That the Father may be glorified in the Son." When we consciously yield ourselves spirit, soul, and body to the inspiration of the Word and Spirit, our desires will no longer be ours. They will be His, and their main purpose will be the glory of God. With increasing liberty we will be able in prayer to say, "Father, You know we ask it only for your glory."

Answers to prayer, instead of being mountains we cannot climb, will give us greater confidence that we are heard. And the privilege of prayer will become doubly precious because it brings us into perfect unison with the beloved Son in the wonderful partnership He proposes: "You ask and I do, that the Father may be glorified in the Son."

162

LORD, TEACH US TO PRAY

Blessed Lord Jesus! Once again I come to you. Every lesson You give me convinces me all the more deeply that I don't know how to pray properly. But every lesson also inspires me with hope that You are going to teach me what prayer should be.

O my Lord! I look to You with courage. You are the great intercessor. You alone pray and hear prayer for the sole purpose of glorifying the Father. Teach me to pray as You do.

Savior! I want to be nothing, yielding myself totally to You. I am giving myself to be crucified with You. Through the Spirit the works of self will be made dead. Let Your life and Your love of the Father take possession of me. A new longing is filling my soul that every day and every hour prayer to the glory of the Father will become everything to me.

O my Lord! Please teach me this.

My God and my Father! Accept the desire of Your child who has seen that Your glory is alone worth living for. "Please, show me Your glory."[14] Let it overshadow me and fill my heart. May I dwell in it as Christ did. Tell me what pleases You, fulfill in me Your own good pleasure,[15] so that I may find my glory in seeking the glory of You my Father. Amen.

NOTES ON LESSON NINETEEN

[1] John 14:12-13

[2] The author's quotation could not be found in any current Bible version, perhaps it is a paraphrase of parts of John 5:30 and 6:38. The former reads, "I do not seek My own will but the will of the Father who sent Me," and the latter reads, "I have come . . . not to do My own will, but the will of Him who sent Me" (NKJV).

[3] John 17:1, 4

[4] Hebrews 4:12

[5] 1 Corinthians 10:31

[6] John 14:13

[7] John 17:4

[8] Ephesians 3:17

[9] Revelation 4:9-11

[10] John 15:8

[11] John 5:44, NRSV

[12] Hebrews 12:2

[13] Ephesians 1:13

[14] Exodus 33:18

[15] Philippians 2:13

PERSONAL NOTES

_____

_____

_____

_____

LESSON 20

THE ALL-INCLUSIVE CONDITION

*"If you abide in Me, and My words abide
in you, you will ask what you desire, and
it shall be done for you."* [1]

In all God's relations with us, the promise and its
conditions are inseparable. If we fulfill the conditions,
He fulfills the promise. What He is to be to us depends
on what we are willing to be to Him: "Draw near to
God, and He will draw near to you." [2] Therefore, in
prayer, the unlimited promise, *Ask what you desire,* has
one simple and natural condition, *if you abide in me.* It
is Christ whom the Father always hears. God is *in
Christ.* [3]

To reach God, we must be in Christ, too. Fully
abiding in Him, we have both the right to ask whatever
we desire and the promise that we will get an answer.

There is a terrible discrepancy between this
promise and the experience of most believers. How

many prayers bring no answer? The cause must be either that we do not fulfill the condition, or God does not fulfill the promise. Believers are not willing to admit either, and therefore have devised a way of escape from the dilemma. They put a qualifying clause into the promise that our Savior did not put there—if it is God's will. This maintains both God's integrity and their own.

If only they would accept the promise and hold fast to it as it stands, trusting Christ to make it true. If only they would confess their failure in fulfilling the condition as the one explanation for unanswered prayer, God's Spirit would then lead them to see how appropriate such a promise is to those who really believe that Christ means it. The Holy Spirit would then make our weakness in prayer a mighty motivation for us to discover the secret and obtain the blessing of fully abiding in Christ.

GOD'S WORD GROWS

As Christians grow in grace and knowledge of the Lord Jesus, they are often surprised to find how God's Word grows, too, into new and deeper meanings. They can look back to the day when some Word of God was opened up to them, and they rejoiced in the blessing they had found in it.

After a time, some deeper experience gave the words a new meaning, and it was as if they never had seen what it contained. And yet once again, as they advanced in the Christian life, the same words stood before them as a great mystery, until the Holy Spirit led them still more deeply into its divine fullness.

The Master's precious "abide in me" is one of these ever-growing, never-exhausted words. Step by step, it opens the fullness of the divine life to us. As the union of the branch with the vine is one of never-ceasing growth, so our abiding in Christ is a life process in which the divine life takes more and more complete possession of us. Young believers [see Endnote[4]] may really be abiding in Christ to the limited extent that is possible for them. If they reach upward to attain what the Master means by *full abiding,* they will inherit all the promises connected with it.

GROWING LIFE OF ABIDING

In the growing life of abiding in Christ, the first stage is that of faith. As new believers see that Christ's command is really meant for them, their great aim is simply to believe that abiding in Christ is their immediate duty and a blessing within their reach. They are especially occupied with the love, power, and faithfulness of the Savior. They feel their one basic need is to *believe.*

It is not long, however, before they see that something more is needed. Obedience and faith must go together. But faith can't simply be added *to* obedience, it must be revealed *in* obedience.

Faith is obedience at home, looking to the Master. *Obedience* is faith going out to do His will.

The privileges and blessings of this abiding are often of more interest than its duties and its fruit. Much self-will passes unnoticed. The peace that young disciples enjoy in believing leaves them. In practical obedience the abiding must be maintained: "If you keep My commandments, you will abide in My love."[5]

Before, the truth that the *mind* believed was enough to let the heart rest on Christ and His promises. Now, in this stage, the chief effort is to get the will united with the will of the Lord, and have the heart and life brought entirely under Christ's rule.[6]

SOMETHING STILL MISSING

Yet there still seems to be something missing. The will and the heart are on Christ's side—the disciples obey and love their Lord. But why does their fleshly nature still have so much power? Why aren't their spontaneous actions and emotions what they should be? Where is the beauty of holiness, the zeal of love, and the conformity with Jesus and His death, in which the life of self is lost? There must surely be something that they have not yet experienced through abiding in Christ.

Faith and obedience are just the pathway to blessing. Before giving us the parable of the vine and the branches, Jesus had very distinctly told what that full blessing is. Three times over He said, "If you love me, keep my commandments" [see Endnote[7]], promising a threefold blessing with which He would crown such obedient love: the indwelling of the Holy Spirit,[8] the manifestation of the Son,[9] the Father and Son coming to make their abode within us.[10]

AS FAITH GROWS INTO OBEDIENCE

As our faith grows into obedience, and as in obedience and love our whole being reaches out and clings to Christ, our inner life opens up. The capacity is formed within us of receiving the life and the Spirit of the glorified Jesus, through a distinct and conscious union with Christ and with the Father. The word is fulfilled in us: "On that day you will realize that I am in my Father, and you are in me, and I am in you."[11]

God and Christ exist in each other, not only in will and in love, but in identity of nature and life. Because of this union between the Father and the Son, we are in Christ and Christ is in us in exactly the same way.

TRUE ABIDING

After Jesus had spoken thus, He said, "Abide in me, and I in you.[12] *Accept, consent to receive that divine life of union with me, in virtue of which, as you abide in me, I also abide in you, even as I abide in the Father. So that your life is mine and mine is yours*" [see Endnote[13]].

True abiding consists of two parts—occupying a position into which Christ can come and abide, and abiding in Him so that the soul lets Him take the place of the self to become our life. Like little children who have no cares, we find happiness in trusting and obeying the love that has done everything for us.

To those who thus abide, the promise, "Ask whatsoever you will" [seen Endnote[14]], comes as their rightful heritage. It cannot be otherwise. Christ has full possession of them. He dwells in their love, their wills, and their lives. Not only have their wills been given up, Christ has entered them, dwelling and breathing there by His Spirit. These people pray in Him, He prays in them, and the Father always hears Him. What they ask will be done for them.

169

ABIDE IN CHRIST

Beloved believer. Let us confess that because we do not abide in Christ as He would like us to, the Church is impotent in the face of infidelity, worldliness, agnosticism, and atheism. In the midst of such enemies, the Lord could make His Church more than a conqueror. We must believe that He means what He promises, and accept the conviction the confession implies.

But don't be discouraged. The abiding of the branch in the vine is a life of never-ceasing growth.[15] The abiding (as the Master meant it) is within our reach, for He lives to give it to us. Let us but be ready to count all things as loss and to say, "What I have attained so far is hardly anything. I want to learn to perceive Christ the same way He perceives me."

Let us not be occupied so much with the abiding as with *Him* to whom the abiding links us and His fullness. Let it be Christ—the whole Christ, in His obedience and humiliation, in His exaltation and power—in whom our soul moves and acts. He Himself will fulfill His promise in us.

As we abide and grow into fuller and fuller abiding, let us exercise our right—the will to enter into God's will. Obeying what that will commands, let us claim what it promises. Let us yield to the teaching of the Holy Spirit. He will show each of us what the will of God is so that we may claim it in prayer.

Let us be content with nothing less than the personal experience of what Jesus gave when He said, "If you abide in Me, and My words abide in you, you will ask what you desire, and it shall be done for you."[16]

LORD, TEACH US TO PRAY

Beloved Lord! Make Your promise in all its simplicity new to us. Teach me to accept it, letting the only limitation on Your holy giving be my own willingness.

Lord! Let each word of Your promise be, in a new way, made quick and powerful in my soul.

You say, abide in me. *O my Master, my life, my all—I do abide in You. Allow me to grow up in all Your fullness. It is not the effort of faith (trying to cling to You and trusting You to protect me), or my will (obeying You and keeping Your commandments), that alone can satisfy me. Only You Yourself, living in me as you do in the Father, can satisfy me. It is You, my Lord, no longer before me and above me, but united with me, that I need. I trust You for this.*

You say, ask what you desire. *Lord, I know that a life of complete, deep, abiding will renew, sanctify, and strengthen my will in such a way that I will have the desire and the liberty to ask for great things.*

Lord! Let my will—dead in Your death, living in Your life—be bold and large in its petitions.

You say, it shall be done for you. *O Lord Jesus, You are the Amen, the faithful and true witness.*[17] *Give me in Yourself the joyous confidence that You will make this promise even more wonderfully true to me than ever before, because it has not entered into the heart of people to conceive what God has prepared for those who love Him.*[18] *Amen.*

171

[AUTHOR'S NOTE]

Many books and sermons on prayer emphasize the blessing of prayer as a spiritual exercise, even if there is no answer. It is true that God's fellowship should be more important to us than the gift we ask for, but a careful examination of what Jesus said about prayer reveals that He wants us to think of prayer more as the means to an end. The answer was to be the proof that we and our prayer are acceptable to the Father in heaven.

It is not that Christ would have us consider the gifts of higher value than the fellowship and favor of the Father. By no means. But the Father intends the answer to be a token of His favor and of the reality of our fellowship with Him.

ANSWERS ARE PROOF OF SPIRITUAL MATURITY

Daily answer to prayer is the proof of our spiritual maturity. It shows that we have attained the true abiding in Christ, and that our will is truly one with God's will. It also reveals that our faith is strong enough to see and take what God has prepared for us, that the name of Christ and His nature have taken full possession of us, and that we have been found fit to take a place among those whom God admits to His counsels—according to whose prayers He rules the world.

Prayer is very blessed, but the answer is more blessed still. It is the response from the Father that shows that our prayers, our faith, and our wills are indeed as He wishes them to be.

ANSWER TO PRAYER MUST BE EXPECTED

I make these remarks with the one desire of leading you to accept the truth that when prayer is what it should be, or rather when we are what we should be, the answer must be expected.

Accepting this will bring us out from those refuges where we have comforted ourselves with unanswered prayer. It will show us the place of power to which Christ has appointed His Church, that place which it occupies so little. It will reveal the terrible weakness of our spiritual life as the cause of our not praying boldly in Christ's name. It will urge us mightily to rise to a life in full union with Christ and in the fullness of the Spirit as the secret of effective prayer.

It will also lead us to realize our destiny: "And in that day . . . Most assuredly, I say to you, whatever you ask the Father in My name He will give you. . . . Ask, and you will receive, that your joy may be full."[19] *Prayer that is really, spiritually, in union with Christ is always answered.*

NOTES ON LESSON TWENTY

[1] John 15:7
[2] James 4:8
[3] Ephesians 4:32
[4] Not necessarily young in calendar years, but young in spiritual years.
[5] John 15:10
[6] Ephesians 3:17
[7] Only one verse containing this exact phrase could be found, John 14:15, but other verses contain phrases close to it, and are associated with the

blessings the author mentions.

8 John 14:15-16

9 John 14:21

10 John 14:23

11 John 14:20

12 John 15:4

13 The italicized section of this quotation cannot be found in the Scriptures, and so is undoubtedly the author's conjecture of what Jesus essentially meant from His statements in several verses.

14 Phrasing is different than in the Scriptures—see John 14:13, 15:16, and 16:23.

15 John 15:1-7

16 John 15:7

17 Revelation 3:14

18 1 Corinthians 2:9

19 John 16:23-24

PERSONAL NOTES

_____

_____

_____

_____

_____

_____

LESSON 21

THE WORD AND PRAYER

*"If you abide in Me, and My words abide
in you, you will ask what you desire, and
it shall be done for you."*[1]

The vital connection between the Word and
prayer is one of the simplest and earliest lessons of
the Christian life. As a newly converted pagan put
it: "I pray—I speak to my Father. I read—my Father
speaks to me."

Before prayer, God's Word strengthens you by
giving your faith its justification and its petition.
After prayer, God's Word prepares you by revealing
what the Father wants you to ask. In prayer, God's
Word brings you the answer, for in it the Spirit
allows you to hear the Father's voice.

PRAYER IS DIALOGUE

Prayer is not monologue, but dialogue—a conversation between two people. Its most essential part is God's voice in response to yours. Listening to God's voice is the secret of the assurance that He will listen to yours: "incline Your ear and hear,"[2] "give ear to me,"[3] and "listen,"[4] are words that God speaks to people as well as people to God. His listening will depend on ours.

Your willingness to accept His words will determine the power your words have with Him. What God's words are to you is the test of what He Himself is to you. It shows the uprightness of your desire to meet Him in prayer.

CONNECTION BETWEEN WORD AND PRAYER

It is this connection between His Word and our prayers that Jesus points to when He says, "If you abide in Me, and My words abide in you, you will ask what you desire, and it shall be done for you." The deep importance of this truth becomes clear if we notice the expression that this one replaces.

More than once Jesus had said, "Abide in me and I *in you*" [see Endnote[5]]. His abiding in us was the complement and the crown of our abiding in Him. But here, instead of "You abide in me and *I in you,*" "He says, "You abide in me and *My words abide in you.*" The abiding of His words is the same as abiding Himself. What a view this opens to us of the place the words of God in Christ are to have in our spiritual lives, especially in our prayer.

IN YOUR WORDS YOU GIVE YOURSELF

In your promise, *you give yourself away,* binding yourself to the one who receives your promise. In your commands, you proclaim your will, seeking to *make yourself leader* of those whose obedience you claim, to guide and use them as if they were part of yourself. Through our words, spirit holds fellowship with spirit. If your words are heard, accepted, held fast, and obeyed, you can impart yourself to someone else through them. But with human beings this can happen only in a limited sense.

IN GOD'S WORDS HE GIVES HIMSELF

God, however, is the infinite being in whom everything is life, power, spirit, and truth, in the very deepest meaning of the words. When God reveals Himself in His words, He does indeed give *Himself*—His love and His life, His will and His power—to those who receive His words, in a reality that surpasses comprehension.

In every promise, God gives us the power to grasp and possess *Him.* In every command, He allows us to share His will, His holiness, and His perfection. God's Word gives us God Himself. That Word is nothing less than the eternal Son, Christ Jesus.[6] Therefore, all of Christ's words are God's words, full of a divine, quickening, life and power. "The words I have spoken to you are spirit and they are life."[7]

SPEAKING DEPENDS ON HEARING

Those who study the deaf and mute tell us how much the power of speaking depends on that of hearing, and how the loss of hearing in children is followed by a loss of speaking, too. This is also true in a broader sense—our speech is based on what we hear. In the highest sense, this is true of our conversation with God.

To offer a prayer—to utter certain wishes and appeal to certain promises—is an easy thing that people can learn with human intelligence. But to pray in the Spirit[8] —to speak words that reach and touch God, affecting and influencing the powers of the unseen world—depends entirely on our hearing God's voice. We must listen to the voice and language that God uses and, through the words of God, receive His thoughts, His mind, and His life into our hearts.

The extent to which we listen will determine the extent to which we learn to speak in the voice and the language that God hears. The ear of the learner, wakened morning by morning, prepares the person to speak to God.[9]

HEARING IS SOMETHING MORE THAN STUDY

This hearing the voice of God is something more than the thoughtful study of the Word. You can study and gain knowledge of the Word and still have little real fellowship with the living God.

But there is also a reading of the Word, in the very presence of the Father and under the leading of the Spirit, in which the Word comes to us in living power from God Himself. It is to us the very voice of the Father—a real, personal, conversation with Him. The living voice of God enters the heart, bringing blessing and strength, and awakening the response of a living faith that reaches back to the heart of God.

POWER TO OBEY AND BELIEVE
DEPENDS ON HEARING

The power both to obey and believe depends on hearing God's voice this way. The chief thing is not knowing *what* God has said we must do, but that *God Himself* says it to us. Neither the Law nor the Book nor the knowledge of what is right works obedience. This can be accomplished only by the personal influence of God through His living companionship.

The presence of *God Himself as* the promiser, not the knowledge of what He has promised, awakens faith and trust in prayer. It is only in the full presence of God that disobedience and unbelief become impossible.

CHRIST GIVES HIMSELF

"If you abide in Me, and My words abide in you, you will ask what you desire, and it shall be done for you." In these words, Christ gives Himself. We must have the words in us—taken up into our wills and lives—reproduced in our inner natures and conduct. They must *abide* [dynamically live] in us. Our lives must be one continuous display of the words that fill us. The words reveal Christ inside and our lives reveal Him outside.

As the words of Christ enter deep into our hearts, becoming and influencing our lives, our words will enter His heart and influence Him.

My prayer depends on my life. Whatever God's words are *to* me and *in* me will determine what my words will be *to* God and *in* God. If I do what God says, God will do what I ask.

179

PRAYERS OF OLD TESTAMENT SAINTS

The Old Testament saints understood this connection between God's words and ours quite well. Their prayer really was a loving response to what they had heard God speak. If the words were a promise, they counted *on God to do as He had spoken.*[10] *"Do* as You have said."[11] "For You, O Lord GOD, have spoken it."[12] "Keep what You promised."[13] "According to Your Word."[14]

In such expressions they showed that what God spoke in promise was the root and the life of what they spoke in prayer. If the word was a command, they simply *did as the Lord had spoken: "So* Abram departed as the LORD had spoken."[15] Their lives were fellowship with God, the exchange of word and thought. What God spoke they heard and did—what they spoke God heard and did.

In each word, God speaks to us, and the whole Christ gives Himself to fulfill it. For each word, Christ asks no less than that we give ourselves wholly to keep that word and to receive its fulfillment.

CONDITION SIMPLE AND CLEAR

"If . . . my words abide in you." The condition is simple and clear. In His words His will is revealed. As the words abide in me, His will rules me. My will becomes the empty vessel that His will fills, and the willing instrument that His will rules. He fills my inner being.

In the exercise of obedience and faith, my will becomes stronger and is brought into deeper inner harmony with Him. Because He can fully trust it to will nothing but what He wills, He is not afraid to give the promise, "if . . . my words abide in you, ask what you desire, and it shall be done for you." To all who believe it and act upon it, Christ will make it literally true.

EXCUSING UNANSWERED PRAYERS

While we have been excusing our unanswered prayers with a fancied submission to God's wisdom and will, the real reason has been that our own feeble lives have been the cause of our feeble prayers. Nothing can make Christians strong but the Word coming from God's mouth. By that we must live. The Word of Christ makes us one with Him and fits us spiritually for touching and taking hold of God. We must love and live in that Word, letting it abide in and become part of us.

All that is of the world passes away—"The grass withers, the flower fades, But the word of our God stands forever."[16] Whoever does God's will lives forever. Let us yield heart and life to the words of Christ, the words in which He gives *Himself,* our personal living Savior. His promise will become our rich experience: "If you abide in Me, and My words abide in you, you will ask what you desire, and it shall be done for you."

LORD, TEACH US TO PRAY

Blessed Lord! I see why my prayer has not been more believing and effective. I was more occupied with my speaking to You than with Your speaking to me. I did not understand that the secret of faith is this—there can be only as much faith as there is of the living Word dwelling in the soul.

Your Word taught me so clearly to be "swift to hear, slow to speak,"[17] and not to be hasty to say just anything to God.

Lord, teach me that it is only when I take Your Word into my life that my words can be taken into Your heart. Teach me that if Your Word is a living power within me, it will be a living power with You, also. Show me that what Your mouth has spoken Your hand will perform.

Lord Jesus! Deliver me from the uncircumcised ear.[18] Give me the opened ear of the learner, wakened morning by morning to hear the Father's voice.[19] Just as You speak only what you hear from the Father, may my speaking be the echo of Your speaking to me.

"When Moses went into the tabernacle of meeting to speak with Him, he heard the voice of One speaking to him from above the mercy seat."[20]

Lord, may it be so with me, too. Let my life and character reveal that Your words abide and are seen in me. May this be my preparation for the complete blessing: "you will ask what you desire, and it shall be done for you." Amen.

NOTES ON LESSON TWENTY-ONE

[1] John 15:7

[2] Isaiah 55:3, Daniel 9:18

[3] Job 34:2, Isaiah 51:4

[4] 2 Chronicles 6:19, Psalm 81:8, Isaiah 46:3,

[5] The exact expression could only be found once, in John 15:4.

[6] John 1:1-2

[7] John 6:63

[8] Ephesians 6:18
[9] Isaiah 50:4
[10] Romans 4:20-21
[11] 2 Samuel 7:25
[12] 2 Samuel 7:29
[13] 1 Kings 8:25
[14] Psalm 119:76
[15] Genesis 12:4
[16] Isaiah 40:8
[17] James 1:19
[18] Jeremiah 6:10
[19] Isaiah 50:4
[20] Numbers 7:89

PERSONAL NOTES

_____

_____

_____

_____

_____

_____

LESSON 22

OBEDIENCE: THE PATH TO POWER IN PRAYER

*"You did not choose Me, but I chose you
and appointed you that you should go and
bear fruit, and that your fruit should
remain, that whatever you ask the Father
in My name He may give you."[1]
The effective, fervent prayer of a
righteous man avails much.[2]*

The promise of the Father's giving whatever we ask is here once again renewed, showing us to whom such wonderful influence in the council chamber of the Most High is to be granted. "I chose you," the Master says, "and appointed you that you should go and bear fruit, and that your fruit should remain." He then adds, *to the end* [or *for the purpose*] *"that* whatever you," (the fruit-bearing ones) "ask the Father in My name, He may give you."

This is nothing but a fuller expression of what He meant by the words, "If you abide in me." He had spoken of the object of this abiding as the bearing of "fruit," "more fruit," and "much fruit."[3] In this, God would be glorified[4] and the mark of discipleship would be seen.

He now adds that the reality of the abiding, as seen in fruit abounding and abiding, is the qualification for praying so as to obtain what we ask. Entire dedication to the fulfillment of our calling is the key to effective prayer and the unlimited blessings of Christ's wonderful prayer-promises.

There are Christians who fear that such a statement is at variance with the doctrine of free grace. But surely it doesn't disagree with free grace rightly understood or the many express statements of God's blessed Word.

WORDS OF JOHN, JAMES, AND THE PSALMS

Take the words of the apostle John, "My little children, let us not love in word or in tongue, but in deed and in truth. And by this we know that we are of the truth, and shall assure our hearts before Him.[5] . . . And whatever we ask we receive from Him, because we keep His commandments and do those things that are pleasing in His sight."[6]

Or take the often-quoted words of James: "The effective, fervent prayer of a righteous man avails much."[7] This describes a person of whom, according to the definition of the Holy Spirit, it can be said, "He who practices righteousness is righteous, just as He is righteous."[8]

Mark the spirit of so many of the Psalms, with their confident appeal to the integrity and righteousness of the supplicant. David says, " The LORD has dealt with me according to my righteousness; according to the cleanness of my hands he has rewarded me[9] . . . I have been blameless before Him and have kept myself from sin. The LORD has rewarded me according to my righteousness, according to the cleanness of my hands in His sight."[10]

If we carefully consider these Scriptures in the light of the New Testament, we find them in perfect harmony with the explicit teaching of the Savior's parting words: "If you keep My commandments, you will abide in My love,"[11] and "You are My friends if you do whatever I command you."[12] The words are indeed meant literally: "I chose you and appointed you that you should go and bear fruit, that, . . . that whatever you ask the Father in My name He may give you." [13]

THE SPIRIT OF THE SAVIOR'S TEACHING

Let us seek to enter into the spirit of what the Savior teaches us here. There is a danger in our evangelical religion of looking too much at what it offers from one side, such as a certain experience obtained in prayer and faith. There is another side that God's Word puts very strongly, that of obedience as the only path to blessing.

What we need to realize is that in our relationship to God He is the infinite being who created and redeemed us. The first sentiment that should motivate us is that of subjection—surrender to His supremacy,

187

His glory, His will, and His pleasure. This should be the first and uppermost thought of our lives.

The question is not, however, how we are to obtain and enjoy His favor, for in this the main thing may still be self. What God in the very nature of things rightfully claims, and is infinitely and unspeakably worthy of, is that His glory and pleasure should be my only object. Surrender to His perfect and blessed will—a life of service and obedience—is the beauty and the charm of heaven.

SERVICE AND OBEDIENCE

Service and obedience were the thoughts that were uppermost in the mind of the Son when He was on earth. Service and obedience must become the chief objects of our desires and aims, even more so than rest, light, joy, or strength. In them we will find the path to all the higher blessedness that awaits us.

Note what a prominent place the Master gives obedience, not only in this fifteenth chapter, in connection with the abiding, but in the fourteenth, where He speaks of the indwelling of the Trinity. John 14:15 says: "If *you* love Me, *keep My commandments,*" and the Spirit will be given to you by the Father. Then verse 21: "He who has My commandments and keeps them, it is he who loves Me." That person will have the special love of the Father and the special manifestation of Christ.

John 14:23 contains one of the highest of all the great and precious promises "If anyone loves Me, *he will keep My word*; and My Father will love him, and We will come to him and make Our home with him."

Could words put it more clearly that obedience is the way to the indwelling of the Spirit, to His revealing the Son within us, and to His preparing us to be the home of the Father? The indwelling of the Trinity is the heritage of those who obey.

OBEDIENCE AND FAITH TWO PARTS OF ONE ACT

Obedience and faith are simply two parts of one act—surrender to God and His will. As faith strengthens itself in order to be obedient, it is in turn strengthened *by* obedience. Faith is made perfect by works.[14]

Often our efforts to believe are unsuccessful because we don't assume the only position in which a large faith is legitimate or possible—that of entire surrender to the honor and the will of God. The person who is entirely consecrated to God and His will finds the power to claim everything that God has promised.

The application of this in the school of prayer is very simple but very solemn. "I chose you," the Master said, "and appointed you that you should go and bear fruit," much fruit,[15] "and that your fruit should remain," that your life might be one of abiding fruit and abiding fruitfulness, "that" as fruitful branches abiding in Me, "whatever you ask the Father in My name He may give you."[16]

TRYING TO PRAY AN EFFECTIVE PRAYER

How often we have tried to pray an effective prayer for grace to bear fruit and have wondered why the answer did not come. It was because we were reversing the Master's order. We wanted to have the comfort, the joy, and the strength first, so we could do the work easily and without any feeling of difficulty or self-sacrifice.

But Christ wanted us to do what He said in the obedience of faith, without worrying about whether we felt weak or strong, or whether the work was hard or easy. The path of fruit-bearing leads us to the place and the power of successful prayer.

OBEDIENCE ONLY PATH TO GLORY OF GOD

Obedience is the only path that leads to the glory of God. Obedience doesn't replace faith or supply its shortcomings. But faith's obedience gives access to all the blessings our God has for us.

In the Gospel of John, the baptism of the Spirit,[17] the manifestation of the Son,[18] the indwelling of the Father,[19] the abiding in Christ's love,[20] the privilege of His holy friendship,[21] and the power of effective prayer,[22] all wait for the obedient.

REASON WE HAVE NOT PRAYED SUCCESSFULLY

Now we know the great reason why we have not had power in faith to pray successfully. Our lives were not as they should have been, Simple obedience— abiding fruitfulness—was not its chief mark.

We wholeheartedly approve of the divine appointment of people to whom God gives the power to rule the world. At their request, He does what otherwise would not have taken place. Their will guides the path in which God's will is to work.

These people must have learned obedience themselves. Their loyalty and submission to authority must be above all suspicion, If we now recognize the law that obedience and fruit-bearing are the path to prevailing prayer, we must with shame acknowledge how little our lives have exemplified this.

YIELD TO SAVIOR'S APPOINTMENT

Let us yield ourselves to take up the appointment the Savior gives us. If we concentrate on our relationship to Him as our Master, we should no longer begin each new day with the thoughts of comfort, joy, or blessing. Our first thought should be: "I belong to the Master." Every moment I must ask His will as His property, as a part of Him, as one who only seeks to know and do His will. I am a servant, a slave of Jesus Christ.

Let this be the spirit that animates us. If He says, "No longer do I call you servants. . . but I have called you friends," let us accept the place of friends, because, "You are My friends if you do whatever I command you."

COMMANDED TO BEAR FRUIT

The one thing He commands us as His branches is to bear fruit.[23] Live to bless others, to testify of the life and the love there is in Christ. In faith and obedience give your whole life to that which Christ chose us for and appointed us to—fruit bearing.

191

Think of His electing us to this, accepting your appointment as coming from Him who always gives us everything He demands of us. We will grow strong in the confidence that a life of fruit bearing and abiding is within our reach. We will understand why this fruit bearing alone can be the path to the place of all effective prayer.

Those who, in obedience to Christ, prove that they are doing what the Lord wills, will receive whatever they desire from the Father. "Whatever we ask we receive from Him, because we keep His commandments and do those things that are pleasing in His sight."[24]

LORD, TEACH US TO PRAY

Blessed Master! Teach me to understand fully what I only partly realize, that only by obeying the will of God can we obtain His promises and use them effectively in our prayers. Show me how bearing fruit perfects the deeper growth of the branch into the Vine, allowing us to experience that perfect union with You and our Father in which we can ask for whatever we want.

O Lord! Reveal to us how with all the hosts of heaven, with all the saints here on earth, and even with You on earth, obedience to God is the highest privilege. Obedience gives access to oneness with the Father Himself in that which is His highest glory—His perfect will. Show us how, if we keep Your commandments and bear fruit according to Your will, our spiritual natures will grow to the full stature of a perfect person,[25] having power to ask and receive anything.

O Lord Jesus! Reveal Yourself to us. Through Your purpose and power, make Your wonderful promises the daily experience of all who completely yield themselves to You and Your words. Amen.

NOTES ON LESSON TWENTY-TWO

[1] John 15:16
[2] James 5:16
[3] John 15:1-5
[4] John 15:8
[5] 1 John 3:18-19
[6] 1 John 3:22
[7] James 5:16
[8] 1 John 3:7
[9] Psalm 18:20
[10] Psalm 18:23-24 — See also Psalms 7:3-5; 15:1-2; 17:3, 6; 26:1-6; and 119:21, 153.
[11] John 15:10
[12] John 15:14
[13] John 15:16
[14] James 2:22
[15] John 15:5, 8
[16] John 15:16
[17] John 14:16
[18] John 14:21
[19] John 14:23
[20] John 15:10
[21] John 15:14
[22] John 15:16
[23] John 15:5
[24] 1 John 3:22
[25] Ephesians 4:13

LESSON 23

THE ALL-POWERFUL PLEA

*"And whatever you ask in My name, that I
will do, . . .
If you ask anything in My name, I will do
it.[1]
. . . that whatever you ask the Father in
My name He may give you.[2]
Most assuredly, I say to you, whatever you
ask the Father in My name He will give
you.
Until now you have asked nothing in My
name. Ask, and you will receive, . . .[3]
In that day you will ask in My name, . . ."[4]*

Until now the disciples had not asked in the name
of Jesus Christ, nor had He Himself ever used the
expression. Here in His parting words He repeats the
expression unceasingly in connection with those

promises of unlimited meaning—*whatever* and *anything*. He wanted to teach them and us that His name is our only—and our completely sufficient—plea. The power of prayer and its answer depend on the right use of the name.

WHAT IS A PERSON'S NAME?

A person's name is a word or expression in which a person is represented to us. When I mention or hear a name, it brings to mind the whole person, what I know of him or her, and also the impression they have made on me. The name of a king or queen includes their honor, their power, and their kingdom. The name is the symbol of the power.

So each name of God embodies and represents some part of the glory of the unseen one. The name of Christ is the expression of everything He has done and everything He is and lives to do as our mediator.[5]

What does it mean to do a thing in the name of another? It is to come with their power and authority, as their representative and substitute. Using another's name always presupposes a common interest. We would not give another the free use of our names without first being assured that our honor and interests were as safe with that other person as with ourselves.

WHAT DOES IT MEAN TO USE JESUS' NAME?

What does it mean when Jesus gives us power over His name—the free use of it—with the assurance that whatever we ask in it will be given to us? The ordinary comparison of one person giving another, on some special occasion, the liberty to ask something in their name, comes altogether short here.

Jesus solemnly gives to all His disciples a general and unlimited power to use His name at all times for everything they desire. He could not do this if He did not know that He could trust us with His interests and that His honor would be safe in our hands.

The free use of someone else's name is always a token of great confidence and close union. Someone who gives their name to another stands aside to let that person act for them. Someone who takes the name of another gives up their own as of no value. When I go in the name of another, I deny myself. I take not only the name, but the person and what that person is, instead of myself and what I am.

A LEGAL UNION

Such use of a person's name may be the result of a legal union. A business owner taking an extensive trip abroad, may give the top official in the business the legal power to disburse whatever funds are necessary to run the business, all in the owner's name. The official does this not for personal reasons, but for the interests of the business. Because the business owner knows and trusts the person as being wholly devoted to the welfare and growth of the business, there is no hesitation about putting his or her name and property at the person's command.

When the Lord Jesus went to heaven, He left His work—the management of His kingdom on earth—in the hands of His servants. He also gave them His name to draw all the supplies they needed for the due conduct of His business. Christ's servants have the spiritual power to use the name of Jesus only insofar as they yield themselves to live only for the interests and the work of the Master—*the use of the name always supposes the surrender of our interests to Christ whom we represent.*

A Life Union

Another use of a name may be because of a life union. (In the case of the business owner and the official, the union is temporary.) Oneness of life on earth gives oneness of name. Children carry the father's family name because they have his life. Often children of a good father are honored or helped by others for the sake of the name they bear. But this would not last long if it were found that it was only a name, and that the father's character wasn't present it in.

The name and the character or spirit must be in harmony. When such is the case, the children will have a double claim on their father's associates, especially close friends. The character secures and increases the love and esteem extended at first for the name's sake.

We are one with Christ—we have one life and one Spirit with Him. For this reason we may proceed in His name.

Our power in using that name, whether with God, people, or demons, depends on the measure of our spiritual life-union with Christ. Our use of His name rests on the unity of our lives with Him.

NAME MEANS NATURE

"Whatever you ask in My name" means "in my nature." With God, things are requested according to their nature. Asking in Christ's name doesn't mean that at the end of some request we say, "This I ask in the name of Jesus Christ." It means we are praying according to His nature, which is love that doesn't seek its own will, but only the will of God and the good of all creatures. Such asking is the cry of Christ's own Spirit in our hearts.

The union that gives power to the use of the name may be the union of love. When a bride whose life has been one of poverty becomes united to an affluent bridegroom, she gives up her maiden name to be called by his family name, and has the full right to use it. Often she purchases in his name for both of them, and he trusts her to do so for his money now belongs to both of them, and each cares as much for the interests of the other as for their own.

The heavenly Bridegroom does nothing less. Having loved us and made us one with Him, what can He do but give those who bear His name the right to present it before the Father for all they need, or go to Him with it for their needs?

We do not really give ourselves up to live in the name of Jesus without receiving in ever-increasing measure the spiritual capacity to ask for and receive in that name whatever we desire. My bearing of the name of another shows that I have given up my own name and, with it, my own independent life. But just as surely it shows I have possession of everything belonging to the name I have taken instead of my own.

NOT PRAYING IN NAME OF ABSENT PERSON

The common comparison to a messenger sent to ask in the name of another, or a guilty person using the name of a guardian in their appeal, is defective—we are not praying in the name of someone who is absent. Jesus Christ is with the Father.

When we pray to the Father, it must be in the name of Jesus Christ. The name represents the person. To ask in His name is to ask in full union of interest, life, and love with Him, as one who lives in and for Him.

SUPREMACY OF THE NAME

Let the name of Jesus have undivided supremacy in your heart and life. Your faith will grow to the assurance that what you ask for in that name cannot be refused.

The name and the power of asking go together. When the name of Jesus Christ has become the power that rules your life, its power in prayer with God will be seen, too.[6]

RELATIONSHIP TO THE NAME

Everything depends on your own relationship to the name. The power it has on your life is the power it will have in your prayers. There is more than one expression in the Scriptures that make this clear.

"Do all in the name of the Lord Jesus"[7] is the counterpart of "ask all [anything]." To do all and ask all in His name go together. "We will walk in the name of the LORD our God for ever and ever"[8] means the power of the name must rule in the whole life. Only then will it have power in prayer.

God looks not to our lips to see what the name is to us, but to our lives. When the Scriptures speak of "those who have given their lives for the name of the Lord Jesus" [see Endnote[9]], or of one "ready . . . to die for the name of the Lord Jesus,"[10] we see what our relationship to the name must be. When it is everything to me, it will obtain everything for me. If I let it have all I have, it will let me have all it has.

WHATEVER YOU ASK IN MY NAME

"Whatever you ask in My name, that I will do." Jesus means that promise literally. Christians have sought to limit it because it looked too free. It was hardly safe for the Lord to trust mortals so unconditionally. They did not understand that the phrase "in my name" is its own safeguard. It is a spiritual power that no one can use further than their way of living and acting in that name allows.

As we bear the name before people, we have the power to use it before God. Let us plead for God's Holy Spirit to show us what the name means, and what the right use of it is. It is through the Spirit that the name, which is above every name in heaven,[11] will take the place of supremacy in our hearts and lives, too.

DISCIPLE OF CHRIST, LEARN THIS LESSON

Let this lesson go deeply into your heart. The Master says, in effect, "Pray in My name, and whatever you ask will be given you." Heaven is opened to you.

The treasures and powers of the spiritual world are placed at your disposal to help those around you.

Learn to pray in the name of Jesus. He says to you, as He said to the disciples; "Until now you have asked nothing in My name. Ask, and you will receive."[12]

As a disciple of Christ, seek to avail yourself of the rights of your royal priesthood, and to use the power placed at your disposal for His work. Awake and hear this message—*your prayers can obtain what would otherwise be withheld.* You can accomplish what would otherwise remain undone.

O awake, and use the name of Jesus Christ to open the treasures of heaven for this perishing world.

LORD, TEACH US TO PRAY

Blessed Lord! It seems as if each lesson You give me has such depth of meaning that if I could learn just that one, I would be able to pray properly. Right now I feel as if I only need to pray for one thing—Lord, please teach me what it is to pray in Your name. Teach me to live and act, to walk and speak, to do everything in the name of Jesus Christ, so that my prayer cannot be anything else but in that blessed name, too.

Lord! Teach me to fully grasp the precious promise that whatever I ask in Your name You will do, and the Father will give. I realize that I haven't fully attained, and that I don't completely understand, the wondrous union you mean when you say, "In My name." Let me hold on to the promise until it fills my heart with the undoubting assurance that I can ask for anything in the name of Jesus.

O my Lord! Let the Holy Spirit teach me this. You described Him as, "the Helper, whom the Father will send in My name" [see Endnote[13]]. He knows what it is to be sent from heaven in Your name, and to reveal and honor the power of that name in Your servants, and to use that name alone to glorify You.

Lord Jesus! Let Your Spirit dwell in me and fill me. I yield my whole being to His rule and leading. Your name and Your Spirit are one. Through Him, Your name will be the strength of my life and my prayer. Then I will be able to forsake everything for Your name's sake, speaking to people and to God in Your name [see Endnote[14]], *and proving that this, indeed, is the name above every name.[15]*

Lord Jesus! Please teach me by Your Holy Spirit to pray in Your name.[16] Amen.

NOTES FOR LESSON TWENTY-THREE

[1] John 14:13-14
[2] John 15:16b
[3] John 16:23-24
[4] John 16:26a
[5] 1 Timothy 2:5; Hebrews 8:6, 9:15, 12:24
[6] Acts 3:6, 16, 4:10, 16:18
[7] Colossians 3:17
[8] Micah 4:5

[9] Acts 15:26 — The verse reads, "men who have risked (hazarded, KJV) their lives for the name of our Lord Jesus Christ."

[10] Acts 21:13

[11] Philippians 2:9

[12] John 16:24

[13] John 14:26 — The seven names usually attributed to the Holy Spirit are: Advocate, Counselor, Comforter, Helper, Intercessor, Standby, and Strengthener.

[14] Acts 4:18, 5:40 — The religious council did not forbid the disciples to teach, they forbid them to teach in the name of Jesus Christ, for they knew that if they could stop the name they could destroy the power of the teaching. It is the same today.

[15] Acts 3:6, 16; 4:7, 10, 12, 16-18; 16:18

[16] James 5:14

PERSONAL NOTES

_____

_____

_____

_____

_____

_____

LESSON 24

THE HOLY SPIRIT AND PRAYER

"And in that day you will ask Me nothing.
Most assuredly, I say to you, whatever
you ask the Father in My name He will
give you.
Until now you have asked nothing in My
name. Ask, and you will receive, that your
joy may be full."[1]
"In that day you will ask in My name, and
I do not say to you that I shall pray the
Father for you;
for the Father Himself loves you, . . ."[2]
But you, beloved, building yourselves up
on your most holy faith, praying in the
Holy Spirit,
keep yourselves in the love of God, . . .[3]

The words of John to little children, young men,
and fathers[4] suggest the thought that often in the
Christian life there are three great stages of experience.

205

1. That of the new-born child, filled with the assurance and the joy of forgiveness.

2. The transition stage of struggle and growth in knowledge and strength, is comparable to young people growing strong. God's Word is doing its work in them and giving them victory over the evil one.

3. The final stage of maturity and ripeness is that of the fathers and mothers, who have entered deeply into the knowledge and fellowship of the Eternal One.

In Christ's teaching on prayer, three similar stages in prayer-life are apparent.

1. The Sermon on the Mount describes the initial stage. All of His teaching is comprised in one word: *Father.* Pray to your Father—your Father sees, hears, knows, and will reward. How *much more* than any earthly father He is. Simply be childlike and trustful.

2. Then comes something like a transition stage of conflict and conquest. Words like these refer to it: "this kind does not go out except by prayer and fasting."[5] "And shall God not avenge His own elect who cry out day and night to Him, . . .?"[6]

3. Finally, we have in Jesus' parting words a higher stage. The children have become adults. They are now the Master's friends, from whom He has no secrets, and to whom He says, "all things that I heard from My Father I have made known to you."[7] In the frequently repeated "whatever you ask," He hands them the keys of the kingdom. Now the time has come for the power of prayer in His name to be proved.

The contrast between this final stage and the previous preparatory ones is marked most distinctly in the words: *"Until now* you have asked nothing in my name,"* and *"In that day* you will ask in My name."

IN THE DAY OF THE HOLY SPIRIT

In that day means the day of the outpouring of the Holy Spirit. The great work Christ was to do on the Cross—the mighty power and the complete victory to be manifested in His resurrection and ascension— would allow the glory of God to come down from heaven as never before, to dwell in people. The Spirit of the glorified Jesus was to come and be the life of His disciples.

One of the signs of that wonderful new flow of the Spirit was to be a power in prayer that was up to that time unknown. Prayer in the name of Jesus Christ— asking for and obtaining everything—is to be the evidence of the reality of the Spirit's indwelling.

The coming of the Holy Spirit began a new epoch in the prayer world. To understand this, we must remember who He is, what His work is, and why His not being given until Jesus was glorified is significant.

It is in the Spirit that God exists, for He is Spirit. It is in the Spirit that the Son was begotten of the Father, because in the fellowship of the Spirit, the Father and the Son are one. The Father's prerogative is eternal, continuous giving to the Son. The Son's right and blessedness is to ask and receive eternally. Through the Spirit, this communion of life and love is maintained. This has been true from all eternity.

THE SON AS MEDIATOR AND INTERCESSOR

It is especially true now, when the Son as mediator lives to pray. The great work that Jesus began on earth of reconciling God and humanity in His own body, He carries on in heaven. To accomplish this, He took the conflict between God's righteousness and our sin into His own person. On the Cross, He ended the struggle once and for all in His own body.[8] Then He ascended to heaven, where He carries out the deliverance He obtained and manifests His victory in each member of His body.

This is why He lives to pray. In His unceasing intercession, He places himself in living fellowship with the unceasing prayer of His redeemed ones. Or rather, it is His unceasing intercession that shows itself in their prayers, giving them a power they never had before.

CHRIST WORKS THROUGH THE HOLY SPIRIT

He does this through the Holy Spirit. This Spirit of the glorified Jesus was not manifested and could not be until Jesus had been glorified.[9] This gift of the Father was something distinctively new and entirely different from what the Old Testament saints had known. The work that the blood effected in heaven when Christ entered within the veil was totally true and new.

The redemption of human nature into fellowship with His resurrection power and His glory was intensely real. The taking up of our humanity through Christ into the life of the triune God was an event of such inconceivable significance that the Holy Spirit was indeed no longer only what He had been in the Old Testament.

HOLY SPIRIT CAME WITH NEW LIFE

That "the Holy Spirit was not yet . . . for Christ was not yet glorified" was literally true. The Holy Spirit had come from Christ's exalted humanity to testify in our hearts of what Christ had accomplished. Just as Jesus, after having come to earth as a man, returned to heaven with power He didn't have before, so the Holy Spirit came to us with a new life that He hadn't had before. He came to us with that new life—as the Spirit of the glorified Jesus.

Under the Old Testament He was invoked as the Spirit of God. At Pentecost He descended as the Spirit of the glorified Jesus, bringing down and communicating to us the full fruit and power of the accomplished redemption.

CHRIST'S CONTINUING INTERCESSION

Christ's continuing intercession maintains the effectiveness and application of His redemption. The Holy Spirit descending from Christ to us draws us up into the great stream of His ascending prayers. The Spirit prays for us without words in the depths of a heart where even thoughts are at times formless.[10] He takes us up into the wonderful flow of the life of the triune God.

Through the Spirit, Christ's prayers become ours, and ours are made His. We ask for what we desire, and it is given to us. We then understand from experience, "Until now you have asked nothing in My name. . . . In that day you will ask in my name."

BAPTISM (OR FILLING) OF THE HOLY SPIRIT

What we need in order to pray in the name of Christ—to ask that we may receive that our joy may be full—is the baptism of this Holy Spirit. This is more than the Spirit of God under the Old Testament. This is more than the Spirit of conversion and regeneration the disciples had before Pentecost.

This is more than the Spirit with a portion of Christ's influence and power. This is the Holy Spirit, the Spirit of the glorified Jesus in His exaltation and power, coming to us as the Spirit of the indwelling Christ,[11] revealing the Son and the Father within us.[12]

This Spirit cannot simply be the Spirit of our hours of prayer. It must be the Spirit of our whole life and walk, glorifying Jesus in us by revealing the completeness of His work and making us wholly one with Him and like Him. Then we can pray in His name, because we are in very deed one with Him. Then we have that immediate access to the Father of which Jesus says, "I do not say to you that I shall pray the Father for you."[13]

Oh, how we need to understand and believe that to be filled with the Spirit of the glorified Christ[14] is the one need of God's believing people. Then we will be able to pray "always with all prayer and supplication in the Spirit,"[15] and "in the Holy Spirit,"[16] and "keep ourselves in the love of God,"[17] "In *that day* you will ask in My name."

THE LESSON LEARNED

Once again, we learn this lesson—*what our prayer achieves depends on what we are and what our lives*

210

are. Living in the name of Christ is the secret of praying in the name of Christ, and living in the Spirit is necessary for praying in the Spirit.

Abiding in Christ gives the right and power to ask for what we desire. The extent of our abiding is equivalent to our power in prayer.

The Spirit dwelling within us prays, not always in words and thoughts, but in a breathing and a being that is deeper than utterance.[18] There is as much real prayer in us as there is of Christ's Spirit.[19] Let our lives be full of Christ and full of His Spirit, so that the wonderfully unlimited promises to our prayers will no longer appear strange.

"Until now you have asked nothing in My name. Ask, and you will receive, that your joy may be full.[20] "In that day you will ask in My name, and I do not say to you that I shall pray the Father for you.[21] Most assuredly, I say to you, whatever you ask the Father in My name He will give you."[22]

LORD, TEACH US TO PRAY

O my God! In holy awe I bow before You, the three in one. Again I see how the mystery of prayer is the mystery of the Holy Trinity. I adore the Father who always hears. I adore the Son who lives eternally to pray. And I love the Holy Spirit who comes from the Father and the Son, lifting us up into the fellowship of that blessed, never-ceasing, asking and receiving. I bow, my God, in adoring worship before the infinite power that, through the Holy Spirit, takes us and our prayers into Your divine life and its fellowship of love.

O my blessed Lord Jesus! Teach me to understand this lesson—the indwelling Spirit streaming from You and uniting us to You is the Spirit of prayer. *Teach me how, as an empty, wholly consecrated vessel, to yield myself to His being my life. Teach me to honor Him and to trust Him, as a living person, to lead my life and my prayer. Teach me especially in prayer to wait in holy silence, giving Him time to breathe His unutterable intercession within me. And teach me that through Him it is possible to pray without ceasing*[23] *and to pray without failing, because He makes me a partaker of the never-ceasing*[24] *and never-failing intercession in which You appear before the Father.*

O Lord! Fulfill me in your promise, "In that day you will ask in My name. Most assuredly, I say to you, whatever you ask the Father in My name He will give you." Amen.

[AUTHOR'S NOTE]

Prayer has often been compared to breathing. We have to carry out the comparison fully to see how wonderful the place is that the Holy Spirit occupies. With every breath, we expel impure air that would soon cause our death, and inhale fresh air to which we owe our life.

In similar fashion, in confession we release our sins, and in prayer we release the needs and desires of our hearts. We inhale the fresh air of the promises, the love, and the life of God in Christ. We do this through the Holy Spirit, who is the breath of our life.

HOLY SPIRIT IS THE BREATH OF GOD

He is also the breath of God.[25] The Father breathes Him into us to unite Himself with our life. Just as every expiration is followed by the inhaling of the next breath, so God inhales His breath, and the Spirit returns to Him laden with the desires and needs of our hearts.

Thus the Holy Spirit is the breath of life of God[26] and the breath of the new life in us. As God breathes Him out, we receive Him in answer to prayer—as we breathe Him back again, He rises to God carrying our petitions.

It is through the Holy Spirit that the Father and the Son are one, and that the intercession of the Son reaches the Father. He is our Spirit of prayer. True prayer is the living experience of the truth of the Holy Trinity. The Spirit's breathing, the Son's intercession, and the Father's will become one in us.

NOTES ON LESSON TWENTY-FOUR

[1] John 16:23-24
[2] John 16:26-27a
[3] Jude 20-21a
[4] 1 John 2:12-14
[5] Matthew 17:21 — The NIV does not contain this verse.
[6] Luke 18:7
[7] John 15:15
[8] Romans 5:10
[9] John 7:39
[10] Romans 8:26
[11] 2 Corinthians 3:17, Galatians 2:20, Colossians 1:27

[12] John 14:16-23
[13] John 16:26
[14] Romans 8:9
[15] Ephesians 6:18
[16] Jude 1:20
[17] Jude 1:21 — with a change in the verse text from "yourselves" to "ourselves."
[18] Romans 8:26
[19] Philippians 1:19
[20] John 16:24
[21] John 16:26
[22] John 16:23
[23] 1 Thessalonians 5:17
[24] Hebrews 7:25
[25] John 20:22
[26] Genesis 7:22; Job 32:8, 33:4, 34:14; Isaiah 42:5

PERSONAL NOTES

_____

_____

_____

_____

_____

_____

LESSON 25

CHRIST THE INTERCESSOR

*"But I have prayed for you, that your
faith should not fail."[1]
"I do not say to you that I shall pray the
Father for you."[2]
He always lives to make intercession for
them.[3]*

All growth in the spiritual life is connected with clearer insight into what Christ is to us. The more I realize that Christ must be everything to me and in me, that everything in Christ is indeed for me, the more I learn to live the real life of faith. This life dies to self and lives wholly in Christ. The Christian life is no longer a vain struggle to live *right,* but a resting in Christ to find strength in Him *as* life. He helps us fight and gain the victory of faith.

THE LIFE OF PRAYER

This is especially true of the life of prayer. It, too, comes under the law of faith alone, and is seen in the light of the fullness and completeness there is in Christ. When seen as such, believers will understand that prayer is no longer a matter of strain or anxious care, but an experience of what Christ will do for them and in them. It is participation in the life of Christ, which is the same on earth as in heaven, always ascending to the Father as prayer. So they begin to pray.

Such believers not only trust the merits of Christ— or His intercession—by which our unworthy prayers are made acceptable, they also trust in that near and close union through which He prays in us and we in Him. Having Him within us, we abide in Him and He in us through the Holy Spirit perfecting our union with Him, so that we ourselves can come directly to the Father in His name.

SALVATION IS CHRIST HIMSELF

The whole of salvation is Christ Himself—He has given *Himself* to us. He Himself lives in us. Because He prays, we pray, too. Just like the disciples, who saw Jesus praying and asked Him to make them partakers of what He knew of prayer, we know that He makes us participate with Him in the life of prayer. He is now our intercessor on the throne.

This comes out quite clearly in the last night of His life. In His high-priestly prayer,[4] He shows us how and what He has to pray to the Father, and what He will pray when He ascends to heaven. He had in His parting address repeatedly connected His going to the

216

Father with *their* new life of prayer. The two—His praying and their praying—would ultimately be connected. His entrance into the work of His eternal intercession would be *the commencement and the power of their new prayer-life in His name.*

CHRIST'S INTERCESSION

It is the sight of Christ in His intercession that gives us power to pray in His name. All right and power of prayer is Christ's—He makes us share in His intercession.

To understand this, think first of His *intercession.* He lives to intercede.[5] The work of Christ on earth as sacrifice for our sins was just a beginning. Aaron offered the blood sacrifice, Jesus shed His blood. Now as a high priest in the order of Melchizedek,[6] He lives within the veil to continue His work for the power of the eternal life.

"It is Christ who died, and furthermore is also risen, who is even at the right hand of God, who also makes intercession for us."[7] That intercession is an intense reality—a work that is absolutely necessary—and without which the continued application of redemption cannot take place. Through the incarnation and resurrection of Jesus, the wondrous reconciliation took place,[8] and we became partakers of the divine life[9] and blessedness.

CHRIST'S DIVINE POWER

But the real, personal, use of this reconciliation cannot take place without the unceasing exercise of His divine power by Christ in heaven. In all conversion and sanctification, in every victory over sin and the world, there is a real exercise of Christ's power.

This exercise takes place through His prayer—He asks of the Father and receives from the Father. "*He is able* to save completely those who come to God through him, *because* he always lives to intercede for them."[10] He receives every need of His people in intercession, extending to them what the Godhead has to give. His mediation on the throne is as real and indispensable as His sacrifice was on the Cross.

Nothing takes place without Christ's intercession. It engages all His time and all His power. It is His unceasing occupation at the right hand of the Father.

WE PARTICIPATE WITH CHRIST

We participate, not only in the benefits of His work, but in the work itself. This is because we are His body. The head and the members are one: "the head cannot say to the feet, "I don't need you!"[11]

We share with Christ everything He is and has. "I have given them the glory that you gave me."[12] We are partakers of His life, His righteousness, and His work. We share His intercession, too. He cannot do it without us.

CHRIST IS OUR LIFE

"Christ who is our life."[13] "I no longer live, but Christ lives in me."[14] The life in Christ and in us is identical—it is one and the same. His life in heaven is a life of continuous prayer. When it descends and takes possession of us, it does not lose its character. It becomes a life of continuous prayer in us, too. It is a life that without ceasing asks and receives from God.

218

This is not as if there were two separate currents of prayer rising upwards—one from Him and one from His people. A substantial life-union is also a prayer-union. What He prays passes through us, and what we pray passes through Him. He is [as] the angel with the golden censer. *"He was given much incense* (the secret of acceptable prayer), *that he should offer it with the prayers of all the saints upon the golden altar."*[15] We live and abide in Him, the heavenly intercessor.

ONLY CHRIST HAS THE RIGHT TO PRAY

The only begotten Son is the only one who has the right to pray. To Him alone it was said, "Ask of Me, and I will."[16] Just as the fullness for all things dwells in Him, a true fullness in prayer dwells in Him, too. He alone has the power of prayer.

Our growth in the spiritual life consists of a deeper belief that all treasures are *in* Him, and that we, too, are *in* Him. We receive each moment what we possess in Him.

Prayer-life is the same. Our faith in the intercession of Christ must not only be in His praying for us when we do not or cannot pray. As the author of our life and our faith, He draws us to pray *in unison* with Him. Our prayer must be a work of faith in the sense that as we know that Christ communicates His whole life in us, He also breathes our praying into us.

To many believers it was a new epoch in their spiritual life when it was revealed to them how truly and entirely Christ was their life, standing responsible for their remaining faithful and obedient. It was then that they really began to live a *life of faith*

No less blessed will be the discovery that Christ is responsible for our prayer-life, too. As the center and embodiment of all prayer, it is communicated by Him through the Holy Spirit to His people [see Endnote[17]].

CHRIST ALWAYS INTERCEDES

"He always lives to intercede for them"[18] as the head of the body. He is the leader in that new and living way[19] which He has opened up as the author and the perfecter [finisher] of our faith.[20] He provides everything for the life of His redeemed ones by giving His own life in them. He cares for their prayer life by taking them up into His heavenly prayer life, giving and maintaining His prayer life within them.

"I have prayed for you," not to render your faith needless, but "that *your faith* may not fail." Our faith and prayer of faith is rooted in His. If we pray with and in the eternal intercessor, abiding in Him, we can ask whatever we will, and it well be done for us.[21]

THE GOAL OF THE PRAYER-PROMISES

The thought of our fellowship in the intercession of Jesus reminds us of what He has taught us more than once before—***all these wonderful prayer-promises have the glory of God, in the manifestation of His kingdom and the salvation of sinners, as their goal.***

So long as we pray chiefly for ourselves, the promises of His last night must remain a sealed book to us. The promises are given to the fruit-bearing branches of the vine, to disciples sent into the world to live for perishing people in the same way as the Father sent Him, to His faithful servants and intimate friends who take up the work He left behind. Like their Lord, they have become seed-corn, losing their lives to multiply them.[22]

Our Prayer Work

Let us each find out what our work is, and which souls are entrusted to our special prayers. Let us make our intercession for them our life of fellowship with God. We will not only discover the truth to the promises of power in prayer, we will begin to realize how our abiding in Christ and His abiding in us makes us share in His own joy of blessing and saving people.

O most wonderful intercession of our blessed Lord Jesus Christ. We not only owe everything to that intercession, but in it we are taken up as active partners and fellow workers. Now we understand what it is to pray in the name of Jesus Christ, and why it has such power.

To pray in His name, in His Spirit, in Him, and in perfect union with Him is the active and effective intercession of Christ Jesus. When will we ever be wholly taken up into it?

Lord, Teach Us to Pray

Blessed Lord! In lowly adoration I again bow before you. All of Your work of redemption has now passed into prayer. You are completely occupied with praying, to maintain and dispense what You purchased with your blood. You live to pray. And because we abide in You, we have direct access to the Father. Our lives can be lives of unceasing prayer, and the answer to our prayer is certain.

Blessed Lord! You have invited Your people to be Your fellow workers in a life of prayer. You have united Yourself with Your people. As Your Body, they share the ministry of intercession with You. Only through this ministry can the world be filled with the fruit of Your redemption and the glory of the Father. With more liberty than ever I come to You, my Lord, and plead with You to teach me to pray. Your life is prayer; Your life is mine. Lord, teach me to pray in You and like You.

O, my Lord, let me know, just as you promised your disciples, that You are in the Father, I am in You, and You are in me. Let the uniting power of the Holy Spirit make my whole life an abiding in You and in Your intercession. May my prayer be its echo, so that the Father hears me in You and You in me. Lord Jesus.

In everything, let Your mind be in me.[23] In everything, let my life be in You. In this way, I will be prepared to be the channel through which Your intercession pours its blessing upon the world. Amen.

NOTES ON LESSON TWENTY-FIVE

[1] Luke 22:23

[2] John 16:26

[3] Hebrews 7:25

[4] John 17

[5] Hebrews 7:25, NIV — Therefore he is able to save completely those who come to God through him, because he always lives to intercede for them.

[6] Hebrews 5:6, 10, 6:20, 7:17

[7] Romans 8:34

[8] Romans 5:11

[9] 2 Peter 1:4

[10] Hebrews 7:25

[11] 1Corinthians 12:21

[12] John 17:22

[13] Colossians 3:4

[14] Galatians 2:20

[15] Revelation 8:3

[16] Psalm 2:7-8

[17] Ephesians 2:18 says, "For through Him we both have access by one Spirit to the Father." The channel of communication is the same in both directions—by or through the Holy Spirit.

[18] Hebrews 7:25

[19] Hebrews 10:20

[20] Hebrews 12:2

[21] John 14:13-14, 15:16, 16:23

[22] John 12:24

[23] 1 Corinthians 2:16

PERSONAL NOTES

_____

_____

_____

_____

_____

LESSON 26

CHRIST THE HIGH PRIEST

After Jesus said this, he looked toward heaven and prayed: "Father, the time has come. Glorify Your Son, that Your Son may glorify You.

"For You granted him authority over all people that he might give eternal life to all those You have given him.

"Now this is eternal life: that they may know You, the only true God, and Jesus Christ, whom You have sent.

"I have brought You glory on earth by completing the work You gave Me to do.

"And now, Father, glorify Me in Your presence with the glory I had with You before the world began.

"I have revealed You to those whom You gave Me out of the world. They were Yours; You gave them to Me and they have obeyed Your word.

"Now they know that everything You have given Me comes from You.

*"For I gave them the words You gave Me
and they accepted them. They knew with
certainty that I came from You, and they
believed that You sent Me.*

*"I pray for them. I am not praying for the
world, but for those You have given Me,
for they are Yours.*

*"All I have is Yours, and all You have is
mine. And glory has come to Me through
them.*

*"I will remain in the world no longer, but
they are still in the world, and I am
coming to You. Holy Father, protect them
by the power of Your name—the name
You gave Me—so that they may be one as
we are one.*

*"While I was with them, I protected them
and kept them safe by that name You gave
Me. None has been lost except the one
doomed to destruction so that Scripture
would be fulfilled.*

*"I am coming to You now, but I say these
things while I am still in the world, so
that they may have the full measure of my
joy within them.*

*"I have given them Your word and the
world has hated them, for they are not of
the world any more than I am of the
world.*

*"My prayer is not that You take them out
of the world but that You protect them
from the evil one.*

*"They are not of the world, even as I am
not of it.*

"Sanctify them by the truth; Your word is truth.
"As You sent Me into the world, I have sent them into the world.
"For them I sanctify myself, that they too may be truly sanctified.
"My prayer is not for them alone. I pray also for those who will believe in Me through their message,
"that all of them may be one, Father, just as You are in Me and I am in You. May they also be in us so that the world may believe that You have sent Me.
"I have given them the glory that You gave Me, that they may be one as we are one:
"I in them and You in Me. May they be brought to complete unity to let the world know that You sent Me and have loved them even as You have loved Me.
"Father, I want those You have given Me to be with Me where I am, and to see my glory, the glory You have given Me because You loved Me before the creation of the world.
"Righteous Father, though the world does not know You, I know You, and they know that You have sent Me.
"I have made You known to them, and will continue to make You known in order that the love You have for Me may be in them and that I myself may be in them."[1]

In His parting address, Jesus gives His disciples the full revelation of what the new life was to be when the kingdom of God had come in power. They were to find their calling and their blessedness in the indwelling of the Holy Spirit, in union with Christ, the heavenly Vine, and in their witnessing and suffering for Him. As He described their future life, the Lord had repeatedly given the most unlimited promises as to the power their prayers might have.

Now in closing, He himself proceeds to pray. To let His disciples have the joy of knowing what His intercession for them in heaven as their High Priest will be, He gives them this precious legacy of His prayer to the Father. He does this because as priests they are to share in His work of intercession, and they must know how to perform this holy work.

PRAYER-PROMISES NOT FOR OUR BENEFIT

In the teaching of our Lord on His last night on earth, recorded in John 17, we recognize that these astonishing prayer-promises have not been given for our benefit, but in the interest of the Lord and His kingdom. Only from the Lord Himself can we learn what prayer in His name is to be and what it can obtain.

To pray in His name is to pray in perfect unity with Him. The high-priestly prayer will teach everyone that prayer in the name of Jesus may ask for and expect everything. This prayer is ordinarily divided into three parts:

1. The Lord prays for Himself (verses 1-5)
2. For His disciples (verses 6-19)
3. For all the believing people of all ages
   (verses 20-26)

The followers of Jesus who give themselves to the work of intercession, and who would like to know how much of a blessing they can pray down upon their circle in the name of Jesus, should in all humility let themselves be led by the Spirit to study this wonderful prayer as one of the most important lessons in the school of prayer.

JESUS PRAYS FOR HIMSELF

First of all, Jesus prays for Himself, for His being glorified, so that He may glorify the Father. "Father, the time has come. Glorify your Son, that Your Son may glorify you."[2] He presents reasons for His praying this way.

A holy covenant was concluded between the Father and the Son in heaven. The Father promised Him power over all flesh as the reward for His work. Now Jesus has done the work, He has glorified the Father, and His one purpose is to further glorify Him. With the utmost boldness He asks the Father to glorify Him, so that He may now be and do for His people everything He has undertaken.

Here you have the first lesson in your work of priestly intercession, to be learned from the example of your great high priest. To pray in the name of Jesus Christ is to pray in unity and in sympathy with Him. The Son began His prayer by clarifying His relationship to the Father, speaking of His work and obedience, and His desire to see the Father glorified.

You should pray like that. Draw near to the Father in Christ. Plead His finished work. Say that you are one with it, that you trust it, and live in it. Say that you, too, have given yourself to finish the work the Father has given you to do, and to live alone for His glory. Then ask confidently that the Son may be glorified in you.

This is praying in the name, in the very words, and in the Spirit of Christ, in union with Christ Himself. Such prayer has power. If with Christ you glorify the Father, the Father will glorify Christ by doing what you ask in His name. It is only when your own personal relationship, like Christ's, is clear with God—when you are glorifying Him and seeking everything for His glory—that, like Christ, you will have power to intercede for those around you.

JESUS PRAYS FOR HIS DISCIPLES

Our Lord next prays for the circle of His disciples. He speaks of them as those whom the Father has given Him. Their distinguishing characteristic is that they have received Jesus' Word.[3] He says He is now sending them into the world in His place, just as the Father had sent Him. He asks two things for them—that the Father would keep them from the evil one, and that He would sanctify them through His Word.

Just like the Lord, each believing intercessor has a personal immediate circle for whom to pray first. Parents have their children, children their parents and other family members, teachers their students, students their school and co-students, employers their employees, employees their co-workers, pastors their congregations, congregations their church and other members, and all believers have those whose care lies

230

on their hearts. It is of great consequence that intercession should be personal, pointed, and definite.

Our first prayer must always be that they receive the Word. But this prayer will not work unless we say to the Lord, "I have given them your Word." This gives us liberty and power in intercession for souls. Don't just pray for them, but speak to them. When they have received the Word, pray for their being kept from the evil one and for their being sanctified through that Word.

Instead of being hopeless or judging, or giving up on those who fall, let us pray, "Holy Father, *protect them* by the power of Your name. *Sanctify them* by the truth; Your word is truth!" Prayer in the name of Jesus Christ accomplishes much: "ask whatever you wish, and it will be given you."[4]

JESUS PRAYS FOR ALL BELIEVERS

Next Jesus prays for a still wider circle: "My prayer is not for them alone. I pray also for those who will believe in me through their message." His priestly heart enlarges itself to embrace all places and all time. He prays that everyone who belongs to Him may everywhere be one, as God's proof to the world of the divinity of His mission. He then prays that they may always be with Him in His glory. Until then, He asks "that the love You have for Me may be in them and that I Myself may be in them."

Disciples of Christ who have first proved the power of prayer in their own circle cannot confine themselves within its limits. They then pray for the universal Church and its different branches. They pray especially for the unity of the Spirit and of love. They pray for its being one in Christ, as a witness to the world that Christ, who has made love triumph over selfishness and separation, is indeed the Son of God sent from heaven. Every believer should pray that the unity of the Church, not in external organizations, but in spirit and in truth, is manifested.

JESUS' PRAYER BASED ON HIS FATHER'S PROMISE

Jesus says, *Father! I want* [*will* or *desire*].[5] Based on His right as Son, the Father's promise to Him, and His finished work, He can do so. The Father had said to Him, "Ask of Me, and I will give You."[6] He now avails Himself of the Father's promise.

Jesus has given us a similar promise, in effect, *"Whatever you desire* will be done for you."[7] He tells you to say in His name what you desire, what you will, what you want. Abiding in Him, in a living union with Him in which you are nothing, and Christ is everything, you have the liberty to take up that word of God's High Priest. In answer to the question, What do you want?[8] say, "Father, I want all that You have promised in Christ's name."

THIS IS TRUE FAITH

Having the confidence to boldly state what you want honors God, and is indeed acceptable to Him. At first sight, our hearts shrink from the expression. We feel neither the liberty nor the power to speak in such a manner. But grace will most assuredly be given to us who lose our will in Christ's will.

Whoever gives up their will entirely will find it again—renewed and strengthened with a divine strength.

FATHER, I DESIRE . . .

"Father, I desire . . ." is the keynote of the everlasting, ever-active, all-powerful intercession of our Lord in heaven. It is only in union with Him that our prayer is effective and accomplishes much. If we abide in Him—living, walking, and doing all things in His name; and take each separate petition, tested and touched by His Word and Spirit, and cast it into the mighty stream of intercession that goes up from Him to be presented before the Father; then we can have full confidence that we have received what we ask for.

The words, "Father, I desire . . ." will be breathed into us by the Spirit Himself. We will lose ourselves in Him and become nothing, finding that in our impotence we have power to succeed.

CALLED TO BE LIKE OUR LORD IN INTERCESSION

We are called to be like our Lord in His priestly intercession.

As the Church of the living Christ, when will we awaken to the glory of our destiny to pray to God for perishing people and be answered?

When will we shake off the sloth that clothes itself in the pretense of humility and yield ourselves wholly to God's Spirit, so that He might fill our wills with the light and power to know, take, and possess everything our God is waiting to give?

233

LORD, TEACH US TO PRAY

O my blessed High Priest! Who am I that You should invite me to share Your power of intercession? And why, O my Lord, am I so slow of heart to understand, believe, and exercise this wonderful privilege to which You have redeemed Your people?

O Lord! Give me Your grace so that my life's work may become praying without ceasing, and thereby draw down the blessing of heaven on all my surroundings on earth.

Blessed Lord! I come now to accept my calling, for which I will give up everything and follow You. Into your hands I will with full faith yield my whole being. Form, train, and inspire me to be one of Your prayer force, those who watch and strive in prayer, who have power and victory.

Take possession of my heart, and fill it with the desire to glorify God in the gathering, sanctification, and union of those whom the Father has given You. Take my mind and give me wisdom to know when prayer can bring a blessing. Take me wholly and prepare me as You would a priest, to stand always before God and to bless His name.

Blessed Lord! Now and through all my spiritual life, let me want everything for You alone, and nothing for myself. Let it be my experience that those who have and ask for nothing for themselves, receive everything, including the wonderful grace of sharing Your everlasting ministry of intercession. Amen.

NOTES ON LESSON TWENTY-SIX

[1] John 17:24
[2] John 17:1
[3] John 15:3
[4] John 15:7b
[5] John 17:24
[6] Psalm 2:8
[7] John 14:13, 15:16, 16:23
[8] Luke 18:41

PERSONAL NOTES

_____

_____

_____

_____

_____

_____

_____

_____

LESSON 27

CHRIST THE SACRIFICE

*"Abba, Father," He said, "everything is
possible for You. Take this cup from me.
Yet not what I will, but what You will."*[1]

What a contrast within the space of a few hours.
What a transition from the quiet elevation of that, "Jesus
lifted up His eyes to heaven, and said . . . Father, I
desire . . ."[2] to that falling on the ground[3] and crying
in agony,[4] "Father, . . . not what I will."

In the one we see the high priest within the veil in
His all-powerful intercession; in the other, the sacrifice
on the altar opening the way through the rent veil. The
high-priestly "Father, I desire" precedes the sacrificial
"Father, not what I will," but this was only to show
what the intercession would be once the sacrifice was
brought.

The prayer before the throne, "Father, I desire," had its origin and its power in the prayer at the altar, "Father, not what I will." From the entire surrender of His will in Gethsemane, the High Priest on the throne has the power to ask what He desires, and the right to make His people share that power, asking what they desire.

THE GETHSEMANE LESSON

For everyone who wants to learn to pray in the school of Jesus, this Gethsemane lesson is one of the most sacred and precious. To a superficial scholar, it may appear to take away the courage to pray in faith. But if even the earnest supplication of the Son was not heard, if even He had to say, "not what I will," how much more we must need to say it.

Because of this, on the surface it appears impossible that the thrice-repeated promise the Lord gave only a few hours previously, "Whatever you ask," could have been meant literally.

A deeper insight into the meaning of Gethsemane, however, would teach us the sure way to the assurance of an answer to our prayers. Gaze in reverent and adoring wonder on this great sight—God's Son praying through His tears, and not obtaining what He asks. He Himself is our teacher and will open up to us the mystery of His holy sacrifice, as revealed in this wondrous prayer.

DIFFERENCES IN JESUS' PRAYERS

To understand the Gethsemane prayer, let us note the infinite difference between what our Lord prayed earlier as royal high priest, and what He here prays in His weakness.

There He prayed to glorify the Father and to glorify Himself and His people as the fulfillment of distinct promises that had been given to Him. He asked what He knew would be according to the Word and the will of the Father. He could boldly say, "Father, I desire . . ."

Here He prays for something in regard to which the Father's will is not yet clear to Him. As far as He knows, it is the Father's will that He should drink the cup. He had told His disciples of the cup He must drink.[5] A little later he would again say, "Shall I not drink the cup the Father has given me?"[6]

It was for this He had come to this earth. But in the unutterable agony of soul that gripped Him as the power of darkness overcame Him, He began to taste the first drops of death—the wrath of God against sin. His human nature, as it shuddered in the presence of the awful reality of being made a curse,[7] gave utterance in this cry of anguish [see Endnote[8]]. Its desire was that if God's purpose could be accomplished without it, He might be spared the awful cup: "Let this cup pass from me" [see Endnote[9]]. That desire was the evidence of the intense reality of His humanity.

NOT AS I WILL

The "Not as I will" kept that desire from being sinful. He pleadingly cries, "everything is possible for You," and returns again to still more earnest prayer that the cup may be removed. "Not as I will,"[10] repeated three times,[11] constitutes the very essence and worth of His sacrifice.

He had asked for something of which He could not say, "I know it is Your will." He had pleaded God's power and love, and had then withdrawn His plea in His final, "Your will be done."[12]

The prayer that the cup should pass away could not be answered. The prayer of submission that God's will be done was heard and gloriously answered in His victory first over the fear, and then over the power of death.

OBEDIENCE AT ITS HIGHEST PERFECTION

In this denial of His own will, this complete surrender of His will to the will of the Father, Jesus' obedience reached its highest perfection. From the sacrifice of His will in Gethsemane, the sacrifice of His life on Calvary derives its value. It is here, as the Scripture says, that He learned obedience[13] and became the author of everlasting salvation to everyone who obeys Him.

Because in that prayer He became obedient until death—the death of the Cross—God highly exalted Him[14] and gave Him the power to ask what He will. It was in the "Father, not what I will,"[15] that He obtained the power for the "Father, I will [desire or want]."

By His submittal in Gethsemane, Jesus secured for His people the right to say to them, "Ask what you desire."[16]

MYSTERIES OF GETHSEMANE

Let us look at the four deep mysteries that Gethsemane offers:

1. The Father offers His well-beloved the cup of wrath

2. The Son, who is always so obedient, shrinks back and implores that He may not have to drink it

3. The Father does not grant the Son His request, and makes Him drink the cup

4. The Son yields His will, is content that His own will is not done, and goes out to Calvary to drink the cup His Father would not remove.

O Gethsemane! In you I see how my Lord could give me such unlimited assurance of an answer to my prayers. He won it for me by His consent to have His petition unanswered.

This is in harmony with the whole scheme of redemption. Our Lord always wins for us the opportunity of what He suffered:

♦ He was bound so that we could go free

♦ He was made sin so that we could become the righteousness of God

♦ He died so that we could live

♦ He bore God's curse so that God's blessing would be ours

♦ He endured God's not answering His prayer, so that our prayers could find an answer

♦ He said, not as I will, so that He could say to us, "If you abide in Me, . . . you will ask what you desire, and it shall be done for you

IF YOU ABIDE IN ME

In Gethsemane the words, "If you abide in Me," acquire new force and depth. Christ is our head, who stands in our place and bears what we would otherwise have had to bear forever. We deserved that God turn a deaf ear to us and never listen to our cries. Jesus came and suffered for us. He suffered what we merited.

For our sins, He suffered beneath the burden of that unanswered prayer. But now His suffering succeeds for me. What He bore is taken away from me.[17] His merit has won for me the answer to every prayer—*if* I abide in Him.

Yes, in Him, as He bows there in Gethsemane, I must abide. As my head, He not only once suffered for me, but He always lives in me, breathing and working His own nature in me.[18] The Spirit through which He offered himself to God[19] is the Spirit that dwells in me, too. He makes me a partaker of the very same obedience and the sacrifice of my will to God.

HOLY SPIRIT TEACHES

The Holy Spirit teaches me to yield my will entirely to the will of my Father, to give it up even unto death. He teaches me to distrust whatever is of my own mind, thoughts, and will, even though it may not be directly sinful. He opens my ear to wait in great gentleness and teachableness of soul for what the Father day by day has to speak and to teach. He shows me how union with God's will—and the love of it—is union with God Himself.

Entire surrender to God's will is the Father's claim, the Son's example, and the true blessedness of the soul.

Holy Spirit Leads

The Spirit leads my will into the fellowship of Jesus' death and resurrection. My will dies in Him, and in Him is made alive again. He breathes into it a holy insight into God's perfect will, a holy joy in yielding itself to be an instrument of that will, and a holy liberty and power to lay hold of God's will to answer prayer.

With my whole will, I learn to live for the interests of God and His kingdom and to exercise the power of that will—crucified but risen again[20]—in nature and in prayer, on earth and in heaven, with people and with God.

The Deeper Life of Gethsemane

The more deeply I enter into the "Father, not what I will" of Gethsemane, and into Him who said it, the fuller is my spiritual access to the power of His "Father, I desire." The soul experiences the reality that the will has become nothing so that God's will may be everything. It is now inspired with a divine strength to really will what God wills, desire what God desires, and to claim what has been promised to it in the name of Christ.

Listen to Christ again as He says, "If you abide in Me, . . . ask what you desire, and it shall be done for you."[21] Be of one mind and spirit with Him in His giving up everything to God's will, and live like Him in obedience and surrender to the Father. This is abiding in Him—and that is the secret of power in prayer.

LORD, TEACH US TO PRAY

Blessed Lord Jesus! Gethsemane was the school where You learned to pray and to obey. It is still Your school, where You lead all Your disciples who wish to learn to obey and to pray just like You.

Lord! Teach me there to pray, with faith that You have atoned for and conquered our self-will and can indeed give us grace to pray like You.

O Lamb of God! I want to follow You to Gethsemane. There I want to become one with You and abide in You, as You to the very death yield Your will to the Father. With You, through You, and in You, I yield my will in absolute and entire surrender to the will of the Father.

Conscious of my own weakness and the secret power with which self will would assert itself and again take its place on the throne, I claim in faith the power of Your victory. You have triumphed over it and delivered me from it. In Your death, I will daily live. In your life, I will daily die. Abiding in You, may my will, through the power of your eternal Spirit, become a finely tuned instrument that yields to every touch of the will of my God. With my whole soul, I say with You and in You, "Father, not as I will, but as You will."[22]

Blessed Lord! Open my heart, and the hearts of all your people, to fully take in the glory of the truth—a will given up to God is a will God accepts for use in His service, and works in so that it desires, determines, and wills what is according to His will.²³ *Let mine be a will that exercises its royal prerogative in prayer, by the power of the Holy Spirit. Let it loose and bind on earth,²⁴ asking whatever it chooses, and saying it will be done.*

O Lord Jesus Christ! Teach me to pray. Amen.

NOTES FOR LESSON TWENTY-SEVEN

¹ Mark 14:36
² John 17:1, 24
³ Matthew 26:39, Mark 14:35
⁴ Luke 22:44
⁵ Matthew 20:22
⁶ John 18:11
⁷ Galatians 3:13
⁸ He who had not known the slightest touch of the foul breath of sin throughout all of eternity would now "be sin for us, so that in Him we might become the righteousness of God." In this lay His horror and His anguish.
⁹ Matthew 26:39 — Jesus' expression as rendered in the KJV, "let this cup pass from me," may have been based upon one of the Romans' methods of executing their own soldiers who had been sentenced to death for various crimes. At times they would line them up on a high cliff and push them over one by one, or if the purpose was simply to instill discipline where it had been lacking in battle, they might push over only selected ones, such as every tenth man. A different method that involved the use of a cup was to line up the men who were to be executed and give the first

man a full cup of hemlock, or some other deadly poison that created great pain in accordance to the amount that he drank. If this first man had the courage, heart, and compassion, he could drink the full measure of the cup, "to its bitter dregs," and suffer all the pains of the poison himself. If he did, the rest of the men would go free. If he did not, the next man must drink the poison also— and he had the same choice as the first man, to drink the full measure of the poison and suffer its pains for the rest of his companions, or he could let them suffer the pains of their portions of the poison. Each man to whom the cup was passed had the same choice. If this was the cup our Lord spoke to His Father about in the Garden, then the symbolism is obvious. (*The New Manners & Customs of the Bible,* James M. Freeman, rewritten and updated by Harold J. Chadwick, copyright © 1998 Bridge-Logos Publishers, North Brunswick, NJ.)

[10] Matthew 26:39
[11] Matthew 26:44
[12] Matthew 26:42
[13] Hebrews 5:8
[14] Philippians 2:9
[15] Mark 14:36
[16] John 15:7
[17] 1 Peter 2:24
[18] Romans 5:10
[19] Hebrews 9:14
[20] Galatians 2:20
[21] John 15:7
[22] Matthew 9:36
[23] Philippians 2:13
[24] Matthew 18:18

LESSON 28

OUR BOLDNESS IN PRAYER

*This is the confidence we have in
approaching God: that if we ask anything
according to His will, He hears us.
And if we know that He hears us—
whatever we ask—we know that we have
what we asked of Him.*[1]

One of the greatest hindrances to believing prayer is this—*many don't know if what they ask is according to the will of God.* As long as they are in doubt on this point, they cannot have the boldness to ask in the assurance that they will certainly receive. They soon begin to think that, once they have made known their requests and receive no answer, it is best to leave it to God to do according to His good pleasure. The words of John, "If we ask anything *according to His will,* He hears us," as they understand them, make certainty of an answer to prayer impossible, because they cannot be sure of what the will of God really may be. They think of God's will as His hidden counsel, and how can mortals know the purpose of a God who is wise in all things?

BOLDNESS AND CONFIDENCE

This is the very opposite of John's purpose in writing what he did—he wanted to stir boldness and confidence in us until we had the full assurance of faith in prayer. He says that we should have the boldness to say to the Father that we know we are asking according to His will, and we know that He hears us.

With such boldness, He will hear us no matter what we ask for, as long as it is according to His will. In faith, we should know that we have the answer. And even as we are praying, we should be able to receive what we have asked.[2]

John assumes that before we pray, we find out if our contemplated prayers are according to the will of God. But even though they may be according to God's will, they may not be answered at once—or they may be other than the persevering prayer of faith. It is to give us courage to persevere and to be strong in faith that He tells us we can have boldness and confidence in prayer, because if we ask anything according to His will, He hears us.

But it is evident that if we are uncertain whether our petitions are according to His will, we cannot have the comfort of His promise, "we know that we have what we asked of Him."

The Difficulty

But this is just the difficulty. More than one believer says, "I do not know if what I desire is according to the will of God. God's will is the purpose of His infinite wisdom. It is impossible for me to know whether He considers something else better for me than what I desire. He may have reasons for withholding what I asked."

We should understand that with such thoughts the prayer of faith becomes an impossibility. There may still be a prayer of submission or of trust in God's wisdom, but there cannot be a *prayer of faith*.

The great mistake here is that God's children do not really believe that it is possible to know God's will. Or if they believe this, they do not take the time and trouble to find it out. What we need is to see clearly how the Father leads His waiting, teachable, children to know that their petition is according to His will. Through God's holy Word—taken up and kept in the heart, the life, and the will—and through God's Holy Spirit—accepted in His dwelling and leading—we will learn to know that what we ask is according to His will.

The Secret Will of God

There *is* a secret will of God, with which we often fear that our prayers may be at variance. But this is not the will of God that we should be concerned with in our prayers. *His will as revealed in His Word* should be our concern. Our notions of a secret will that makes decrees, rendering the answers to our prayers impossible, are erroneous.

Childlike faith in what He is willing to do for His children simply accepts the Father's assurance that it is His will to hear prayer and to do what faith in His Word desires and accepts. In the Word, the Father has revealed in general promises the great principles of His will with His people. We have to take the general promise and apply it to the special circumstances in our life to which it has reference. Whatever we ask within the limits of that revealed will, we may confidently expect, knowing it to be according to the will of God.

GOD REVEALS HIS WILL IN HIS WORD

In His Word, God has given us the revelation of His will. He shows us His plans for us, His people, and for the world. With the most precious promises of grace and power, He carries out these plans through His people. As faith becomes strong and bold enough to claim the fulfillment of the general promise in the specific case, we may have the assurance that our prayers are heard, because they are according to God's will.

Take the words of John in the verse following our text-verse as an illustration: "If anyone sees his brother commit a sin that does not lead to death, he should pray and God *will give him life*."[3] This is the general promise. Believers who plead on the grounds of this promise pray according to the will of God, and John wants them to feel the boldness to know that they have the petition for which they ask.

God's will is something spiritual and must be spiritually discerned. It is not a matter of logic that we can argue about. Not every Christian has the same gift

250

or calling. While God's general will revealed in the promises is the same for everyone, each person has a specific, individual role to fulfill in God's purpose.

The wisdom of the saints is in knowing this specific will of God according to the measure of grace given us, and to ask in prayer just what God has prepared and made possible for each. The *Holy Spirit dwells* in us to communicate this wisdom. The personal application of the general promises of the Word to our specific personal needs is given to us by the leading of the Holy Spirit.

THE WORD AND THE SPIRIT

It is this union of the teaching of the Word and the Spirit that many do not understand. This causes a twofold difficulty in knowing what God's will may be. Some seek the will of God in an inner feeling or conviction, and expect the Spirit to lead them without the Word. Others seek it in the Word, without the living leading of the Holy Spirit. The two must be united.

Only in the Word *and* in the Spirit can we know the will of God and learn to pray according to it. In the heart, the Word and Spirit must meet. Only by their indwelling can we experience their teaching. The Word must abide in us[4] —our heart and life must be under its influence daily.

The quickening of the Word by the Spirit comes from within, not from without. Only those who yield themselves entirely to the supremacy of the Word and the will of God can expect to discern what that Word and will permit them to ask boldly in specific cases.

The same is true of the Spirit. If I desire His leading in prayer to assure me what God's will is, my whole life must be yielded to that leading. Only in this way can mind and heart become spiritual and capable of knowing God's holy will. Those who through Word and Spirit *live in the will of God by doing it*, will know to pray according to that will in the confidence that He hears.

CHRISTIANS DO THEMSELVES INCALCULABLE HARM

If only Christians could see what incalculable harm they do themselves by thinking that because their prayer is possibly not according to God's will, they must be content without an answer. God's Word tells us that the great reason for unanswered prayer is that we do not pray right: "You ask and do not receive, because you ask amiss."[5]

In not granting an answer, the Father tells us that there is something wrong in our praying. He wants us to discover it and confess it, and so teach us true believing and effective prayer. He can only attain this object when He brings us to the place where we see that we are to blame for the withholding of the answer. Our aims, our faith, or our lives are not what they should be. God is frustrated in answering as long as we are content to say: "Perhaps it is because my prayer is not according to His will that He does not hear me."

DO NOT BLAME GOD'S SECRET WILL

O let us no longer throw the blame for our unanswered prayers on the secret will of God, but on our own faulty praying. Let that word, "You ask and do not receive, because you ask amiss," be the lamp of the Lord, searching the inner depths of our hearts[6] to prove that we are indeed those to whom Christ gave His promises of certain answers. Let us believe that we can *know* if our prayers are according to God's will. Let us yield our hearts to the indwelling of the Word of the Father, to have Christ's Word abiding in us.

We should live day by day with the anointing that teaches all things. If we yield ourselves unreservedly to the Holy Spirit as He teaches us to abide in Christ and to dwell in the Father's presence, we will soon understand how our Father's love longs for us to know His will. In the confidence that His will includes everything His power and love have promised to do, we should know, too, that He hears all of our prayers. "This is the confidence [boldness, NRSV] we have in approaching God: that if we ask anything according to His will, He hears us."[7]

LORD, TEACH US TO PRAY

Blessed Master! With my whole heart I thank you for the blessed lesson that the path to a life full of answers to prayer is through the will of God.

Lord! Teach me to know this blessed will by living it, loving it, and always doing it. In this way, I will learn to offer prayers according to that will. In their harmony with God's blessed will, I will find boldness in prayer and confidence in accepting the answer.

Father! It is Your will that Your child should enjoy Your presence and blessing. It is Your will that everything in Your child's life should be in accordance with Your will, and that the Holy Spirit should work this in us. It is Your will that Your child should live in the daily experience of distinct answers to prayer, in order to enjoy living and direct fellowship with You. It is Your will that Your name should be glorified in and through Your children, and that it will be in those who trust You.

O my Father! Let this will of Yours be my confidence in everything I ask.

Blessed Savior! Teach me to believe in the glory of God's will. That will is the eternal love that works with divine power to accomplish its purpose in each human will that yields itself to it.

Lord! Teach me this. You can make me see how every promise and every command of the Word is indeed the will of God, and that its fulfillment is given to me by God Himself. Let His will become the sure rock on which my prayer and my assurance of an answer always rest. Amen.

[AUTHOR'S NOTE]

There is often great confusion as to the will of God. People think that what God wills must inevitably take place. This is by no means the case. God wills a great deal of blessing to His people that never comes to them. He wills it most earnestly, but *they do not will it.* Hence, it cannot come to them.

CREATED WITH FREE WILL

This is the great mystery of our being created with a free will and the renewal of our will in redemption.

God has made the execution of His will dependent on our will. God's will as revealed in His promises will be fulfilled as much as our faith allows.

Prayer is the power by which something comes to pass that otherwise would not have taken place. Faith is the power that determines how much of God's will is done in us. Once God reveals to us what He is willing to do, the responsibility for the execution of His will rests with us.

POWER IN THE HANDS OF MORTALS

Some are afraid that this is putting too much power into the hands of mortals. But all power is put into our hands through Christ Jesus.[8] The key to all prayer and all power is His. When we learn to understand that He is just as much one with us as with the Father, we see how natural, right, and safe it is that such power is given.

Christ the Son has the right to ask whatever He chooses. Through our abiding in Him and His abiding in us, His Spirit breathes in us what He wants to ask and obtain through us. We pray in His name. As we do, the prayers are as much ours as they are His.

FEAR THAT PRAYER LIMITS GOD'S LIBERTY

Others fear that to believe that prayer has such power limits the liberty and the love of God. O if we only knew how we are limiting His liberty and His love by not allowing Him to act in the only way in which He chooses to act, now that He has taken us up into fellowship with Him.

Our prayers are like pipes, through which water is carried from a large mountain stream to a town some distance away. The water pipes do not make the water willing to flow down from the hills, nor do they give it its power of blessing and refreshment. That is its very nature. All the pipes do is to determine the direction.

NATURE OF GOD TO LOVE AND BLESS

In the same way, the very nature of God is to love and to bless. His love longs to come down to us with its quickening and refreshing streams. But He has left it to prayer to say where the blessing is channeled. He has committed it to His believing people to bring the living water to the desert places.

The will of God to bless is dependent on the will of His children to say where the blessings go.

NOTES ON LESSON TWENTY-EIGHT

[1] 1 John 5:14-15
[2] Mark 11:24
[3] 1 John 5:16
[4] John 15:7
[5] James 4:3
[6] Proverbs 20:27
[7] 1 John 5:13
[8] Luke 10:19

LESSON 29

THE MINISTRY OF INTERCESSION

A holy priesthood, to offer up spiritual
sacrifices acceptable to God by Jesus
Christ.[1]
You shall be named the priests of the
LORD.[2]

"The Spirit of the Lord GOD is upon Me, Because
the LORD has anointed Me."[3] These are the words of
the prophet Isaiah that Jesus quoted when "He went
into the synagogue on the Sabbath day."[4] As the fruit
of His work, all redeemed ones are priests—partakers
with Him of His anointing with the Spirit as High Priest.
This anointing is "like the precious oil upon the head,
Running down on the beard, The beard of Aaron,
Running down on the edge of his garments."[5]

Like every son of Aaron, every member of Jesus'
body has a right to the priesthood [see Endnote[6]]. But

not everyone exercises it. Many are still entirely ignorant of it. Yet it is the highest privilege of a child of God, the mark of greatest nearness and likeness to Him who "always lives to make intercession."[7] Do you doubt this? Think of what constitutes priesthood.

THE WORK OF THE PRIESTHOOD

First, there is the work of the priesthood. This has two sides: one towards God, the other towards people. "Every high priest chosen from among mortals is put in charge of things pertaining to God on their behalf.[8] Or, as it is said by Moses, "the LORD separated the tribe of Levi to . . . stand before the LORD to minister to Him and to bless in His name."[9]

On the one hand, the priest had the power to draw near to God, to dwell with Him in His tabernacle, and to present Him with the blood of the sacrifice or the burning incense. This work was not done, however, on the priests' own behalf, but for the sake of the people whose representatives they were. This is the other side of their work. They received people's sacrifices, presented them to God, and then came out to bless in His name, giving the assurance of His favor and teaching the people His law.

Priest are thus people who do not live for themselves. *They live with God and for God.* Their work as God's servants is to care for His house, His honor, and His worship, making known to people His love and His *will. They live with people and for people.*[10] Their work is to find out the people's sins and needs, bring these before God, offer sacrifice and incense in their names, obtain forgiveness and blessing for them, and then come out of the inner place and bless them in God's name.

This is the high calling of every believer. They have been redeemed with the one purpose of being God's priests in the midst of the perishing millions around them. In conformity to Jesus, the great High Priest, they are to be the ministers and stewards of the grace of God.

THE WALK OF THE PRIESTHOOD

Second, there is *the walk of the priesthood,* which is in harmony with its work. As God is holy, so priests were to be especially holy. This means not only separated from everything unclean, but *holy unto God*—being set apart and given up to God for His use. Separation from the world and being given up to God were indicated in many ways.

It was seen in the clothing. The holy garments, made according to God's own orders, marked the priests as His.[11] It was seen in the command as to their special purity and freedom from all contact with death and defilement.[12]

Much that was allowed to an ordinary Israelite was forbidden to them. Priests could have no bodily defects or blemishes.[13] Bodily perfection was to be the model of wholeness and holiness in God's service. The priestly tribes were to have no inheritance with the other tribes—God was to be their inheritance.[14] Their life was to be one of faith—being set apart unto God, they were to live *on* Him as well as *for* Him.

All this is symbolic of what the character of New Testament priests is to be. Our priestly power with God depends on our personal life and walk. Jesus must be able to say of our walk on earth, "They have not defiled their garments."[15]

In our separation from the world, we must prove that our desire to be "holy to the Lord"[16] is wholehearted and entire. The bodily perfection of the priest must have its counterpart in our being "without spot and blameless."[17] We must be "a glorious church, not having spot or wrinkle or any such thing,"[18] " thoroughly equipped for every good work,"[19] and "perfect and complete, lacking nothing."[20]

Above all, we must consent to give up all inheritance on earth. We must forsake everything and—like Christ—have need only of God and keep everything for Him alone. This marks the true priests, the ones who only live for God and for others.

THE WAY TO THE PRIESTHOOD

Third, there is *the way to the priesthood.* God had chosen all of Aaron's sons to be priests. Each of them was a priest by birth. Yet he could not begin his work without a special act of ordinance-his consecration. Every child of God is a priest by right of birth—our blood relationship to the great High Priest. But we can exercise our [priestly] power only as we accept and realize our consecration.

With Aaron and his sons it took place in this manner, as recorded in Exodus 29:

> *After being washed and clothed, they*
> *were anointed with the holy oil.*
> *Sacrifices were then offered, and the*
> *right ear, the right hand, and the right*
> *foot were touched with the blood. They*
> *and their garments were then sprinkled*
> *with the blood and the oil together.*

In the same way, as the blood and the Spirit work more fully in us, the children of God, the power of the holy priesthood will also work in us. The blood will take away all sense of unworthiness, and the Spirit will take away all sense of unfitness.

Notice what was new in the application of the blood to the [Old Covenant] priest. If he had ever as a penitent sought forgiveness by bringing a sacrifice for his sin, the blood was sprinkled on the altar, but not on his person. But now, for priestly consecration, there was to be closer contact with the blood. The ear, hand, and foot were by a special act brought under its power, and the whole being sanctified for God.

The Power of the Blood Cleanses

When believers are led to seek full priestly access to God, they feel the need of a fuller and more enduring experience of the power of the blood. Where they had previously been content to have the blood sprinkled only on the mercy seat as what they needed for pardon, they now need a more personal sprinkling and cleansing of the heart from an evil conscience.[21]

Through this sprinkling, they have "no more conscience of sins"[22] —they are cleansed from all sin. As they begin to experience this, they consciousness is awakened to the full assurance that their intercessions are acceptable.

The Spirit Gives Power
for Intercession

As the blood gives the right, the Spirit gives the power for believing intercession. He breathes into us the priestly spirit and a burning love for God's honor and the saving of souls. He makes us one with Christ to the extent that prayer in His name is a reality. The more Christians are truly filled with the Spirit of Christ, the more spontaneous will be their giving themselves up to the life of priestly intercession.

GOD AND THE WORLD NEED PRIEST

God needs priests who can draw close to Him, live in His presence, and by their intercession draw down the blessings of His grace on others. The world needs priests who will bear the burden of the perishing ones and intercede on their behalf.

Are you willing to offer yourself for this holy work? You know the surrender it demands—nothing less than the Christ-like giving up of everything, so that the salvation of God's love may be accomplished among humanity. Don't be one of those who are content with being saved, just doing enough work to keep themselves warm and lively. Let nothing keep you back from giving yourself to be wholly and only a priest of the Most High God.

NOTHING NEED KEEP YOU BACK

The thought of unworthiness or of unfitness need not keep you back. In *the blood,* the objective power of the perfect redemption works in you. In *the Spirit,* the full, subjective, personal experience of a divine life is secured. *The blood* provides an infinite worthiness to make your prayers acceptable. *The Spirit* provides a divine fitness, teaching you to pray exactly according to the will of God.

Every [Old Covenant] priest knew that when he presented a sacrifice according to the law of the sanctuary, it was accepted. Under the covering of the blood and the Spirit, you have the assurance that all the wonderful promises of prayer in the name of Jesus Christ[23] will be fulfilled in you. Abiding in union with the Great High Priest, "whatever you ask the Father in My name He will give you."[24]

You will have the power to pray the effective prayer of the righteous person that accomplishes a great deal.[25] You will not only join in the general prayer of the Church for the world, but be able in your own sphere to take up your own special work in prayer. As a priest, you will work on a personal basis with God to receive and know the answer, and so bless His name.

BE A PRIEST

Be a priest, only a priest, and all priest. Walk before the Lord in the full consciousness that you have been set apart for the holy ministry of intercession. This is the true blessedness of conformity to the image of God's Son.

LORD, TEACH US TO PRAY

O my blessed High Priest. Accept the consecration in which my soul responds to Your message. I believe in the holy priesthood of Your saints. I believe that I am a priest, having the power to appear before the Father in prayer that will bring down many blessings on the perishing souls around me.

263

I believe in the power of Your precious blood to cleanse me from all sin. It gives me perfect confidence in God and brings me near to Him in the full assurance of faith that my intercession will be heard.

I believe in the anointing of the Holy Spirit. That anointing comes down to me daily from You, my Great High Priest, to sanctify me. It fills me with the consciousness of my priestly calling and with the love of souls. It also teaches me what is according to God's will and how to pray the prayer of faith.

I believe that, just as You are in all things in my life, You are in my prayer life, drawing me up into the fellowship of Your wondrous work of intercession.

In this faith, I yield myself today to my God as one of His anointed priests. I stand before Him to intercede on behalf of sinners, and then return to bless them in His name.

Holy Lord Jesus! Accept and seal my consecration. Lay Your hands on me and consecrate me Yourself to this holy work. Let me walk among people with the consciousness and the character of a priest of the Most High God.

And to You who loved us—who washed us from our sins in Your own blood, and who made us kings and priests before God, Your Father—to You be glory and power forever. Amen.

NOTES ON LESSON TWENTY-NINE

[1] 1 Peter 2:5
[2] Isaiah 61:6
[3] Isaiah 61:1
[4] Luke 4:16-18
[5] Psalm 133:2
[6] For an in-depth study, see *The Priesthood of the Believer* by Dr. Sam Sasser and Judson Cornwall, copyright © 1999 by Judson Cornwall, published by Bridge-Logos Publishers, North Brunswick, NJ.
[7] Hebrews 7:25
[8] Hebrews 5:1, NSRV
[9] Deuteronomy 10:8, 21:5
[10] Hebrews 5:2
[11] Exodus 28
[12] Leviticus 21:1, 11
[13] Leviticus 21:17
[14] Deuteronomy 10:9, 18:1; Joshua 13:14, 33
[15] Revelation 3:4
[16] 2 Chronicles 35:3
[17] 2 Peter 3:14
[18] Ephesians 5:27
[19] 2 Timothy 3:17
[20] James 1:4
[21] Hebrews 10:22
[22] Hebrews 10:2
[23] Acts 3:6, 4:10, 16:18; 1 Corinthians 1:2
[24] John 16:23
[25] James 5:16b

LESSON 30

A LIFE OF PRAYER

Rejoice always,
pray without ceasing,
in everything give thanks; for this is the
will of God in Christ Jesus for you.[1]

Our Lord told the parable of the widow and the unjust judge to teach us that people should pray without ceasing.[2] The widow persevered in seeking one definite thing. The parable appears to refer to persevering in prayer for some special blessing, when God delays or appears to refuse. The Epistles, which speak of continuing in prayer, watching for the answer, and praying always in the Spirit,[3] appear to refer to something different—the whole life being one of prayer. As the soul longs for the manifestation of God's glory to us, in us, through us, and around us, the innermost life of the soul is continually rising upward in dependence, faith, longing desire, and trustful expectation.

WHAT IS NEEDED TO LIVE A LIFE OF PRAYER?

The first thing needed to live a life of prayer is undoubtedly an entire sacrifice of one's life to God's kingdom and glory. If you try to pray without ceasing because you want to be very pious and good, you will never succeed. Yielding ourselves to live for God and His honor enlarges the heart and teaches us to regard everything in the light of God and His will. We instinctively recognize in everything around us the need for God's help and blessing and an opportunity for glorifying Him.

Everything is weighed and tested by the one thing that fills the heart—the glory of God. The soul has learned that only what is of God can really glorify Him. Through the heart and soul, the whole life becomes a looking up, a crying from the innermost heart for God to prove His power and love, and to reveal His glory.

The believers awake to the consciousness that each of them is one of the sentinels on Zion's walls,[4] whose call really does touch and move the King in heaven to do what would otherwise not be done. They understand how real Paul's exhortation was: "praying always with all prayer and supplication in the Spirit, . . . for all the saints; and for me,"[5] and "Continue earnestly in prayer, . . . meanwhile praying also for us."[6] To forget oneself—to live for God and His kingdom among humanity—is the way to learn to pray without ceasing.

CONFIDENCE AND ASSURANCE IN PRAYER

This life devoted to God must be accompanied by the deep confidence that our prayers are effective. In

His prayer lessons, our blessed Lord insisted on faith in the Father as a God who most certainly does what we ask. "Ask, and you will receive."[7] To count confidently on an answer is the beginning and the end of His teaching.[8]

As we gain the assurance that our prayers are effective and that God does what we ask, we dare not neglect the use of this wonderful power. Our souls should turn wholly to God, and our lives should become prayer. The Lord needs and takes time, because we and everyone around us are creatures of time, subject to the law of growth.

But know that not one single prayer of faith can possibly be lost, and that sometimes there is a necessity for accumulating prayer. Know that persevering prayer pleases God. Prayer becomes the quiet, persistent, living of our life of desire and faith in the presence of our God.

DO NOT LIMIT GOD'S PROMISES

Do not limit such free and sure promises of the living God with your reasoning any longer. Don't rob them of' their power, and ourselves of the wonderful confidence they are meant to inspire. The hindrance is not in God, not in His secret will, and not in the limitations of His promises. It is in us. We are not what we should be to obtain the promise.

Open your whole heart to God's words of promise in all their simplicity and truth. They will search us and humble us. They will lift us up and make us glad and strong. To the faith that knows it gets what it asks for, prayer is not a work or a burden, but a joy and a triumph. It becomes a necessity and a second nature.

THE HOLY SPIRIT WITHIN US

This union of strong desire and firm confidence is nothing but the life of the Holy Spirit within us. The Holy Spirit dwells in us, hides Himself in the depths of our being, and stirs our desire for the unseen and the Divine God Himself. It is always the Holy Spirit who draws out the heart to thirst for God and to long for His being recognized and glorified.

Sometimes the Holy Spirit speaks through us in groanings that cannot be uttered,[9] sometimes in clear and conscious assurance, sometimes in distinct petitions for the deeper revelation of Christ to ourselves, and sometimes in pleas for a soul, a work, the Church or the world. When the children of God really live and walks in the Spirit—when they are not content to remain carnal, but try to be fit, spiritual organs for the divine Spirit to reveal the life of Christ and Christ Himself—then the never ceasing life of intercession of the blessed Son must reveal and repeat itself.

Because it is the Spirit of Christ who prays in us, our prayers must be heard. Because it is we who pray in the Spirit, there is need of time, patience, and continual renewing of the prayer until every obstacle is conquered, and the harmony between God's Spirit and ours is perfect.

THE CHIEF THING WE NEED

The chief thing we need for a life of unceasing prayer is to know that Jesus teaches us to pray. We have begun to understand a little of what His teaching is. It is not the communication of what His teaching is. It is not the communication of new thoughts or views, the discovery of failure or error, nor the arousal of desire and faith, however important all this may be.

Jesus' teaching takes us up into the fellowship of His own prayer-life before the Father. This is how Jesus Christ really teaches. It was the sight of Jesus praying that made the disciples ask to be taught to pray. The faith of Jesus' continuous prayer truly teaches us to pray.

We know why: *He who prays is our head and our life.* All He has is ours and is given to us when we give ourselves completely to Him. By His blood, He leads us into the immediate presence of God. The inner sanctuary is our home—we live there. Living so close to God and knowing we have been taken there to bless those who are far away, we cannot help but pray.

WE ARE MADE PARTAKERS

Christ makes us partakers with Him of His prayer power and prayer-life. Our true aim must not be to work a great deal and pray just enough to keep the work right. We should pray a great deal and then work enough for the power and blessing obtained in prayer to find its way through us to people. Christ lives to pray eternally—He saves and reigns. He communicates His prayer-life to us and maintains it in us if we trust Him. He is responsible for our praying without ceasing.

Christ teaches us to pray by showing us how He does it, by doing it in us, and by leading us to do it in Him and like Him. Christ is everything—the life and the strength—for a never-ceasing prayer-life. Seeing Christ's continuous praying as our life, enables us to pray without ceasing Because His priesthood is the power of an endless life—that resurrection life that never fades and never fails. And because His life is our life, praying without ceasing can become the joy of heaven here on earth.

The apostle Paul says, "Rejoice *always*, pray *without ce*asing, in *everything* give thanks."[10] Supported by never-ceasing joy and never-ceasing praise, never-ceasing prayer is the manifestation of the power of the eternal life where Christ always prays.

UNION BETWEEN VINE AND BRANCH

The union between the Vine and the branch is indeed a prayer union. The highest conformity to Christ—the most blessed participation in the glory of His heavenly life—is that we take part in His work of intercession. He *and we* live forever to pray. In union with Him, praying without ceasing becomes a possibility—a reality, the holiest and most blessed part of our holy and blessed fellowship with God.

We abide within the veil in the presence of the Father. What the Father says, we do. What the Son asks, the Father does. Praying without ceasing is the earthly manifestation of heaven, a foretaste of the life where they rest neither day nor night in their song of worship and adoration.[11]

LORD, TEACH US TO PRAY

O my Father! With my whole heart I praise you for this wondrous life of continuous prayer, continuous fellowship, continuous answers, and continuous oneness with Him who lives to pray forever.

O my God! Keep me abiding and walking in the presence of Your glory, so that prayer may be the spontaneous expression of my life with You.

Blessed Savior! With my whole heart I praise You for coming from heaven to share my needs and my pleas, so that I could share Your all-powerful intercession. Thank you for taking me into Your school of prayer, teaching me the blessedness and the power of a life that is totally comprised of prayer. And most of all, thank You for taking me up into the fellowship of Your life of intercession. Now through me, too, your blessings can be dispensed to those around me.

Holy Spirit! With deep reverence I thank You for Your work in me. Through You I am lifted up into communication with the Son and the Father, entering the fellowship of the life and love of the Holy Trinity.

Holy Spirit of God! Perfect your work in me. Bring me into perfect union with Christ, my intercessor. Let Your unceasing indwelling make my life one of unceasing intercession. And let my life unceasingly glorify the Father and bless those around me. Amen.

NOTES ON LESSON THIRTY

[1] 1 Thessalonians 5:16-18
[2] Luke 18:1-8
[3] Ephesians 6:18, Jude 1:20
[4] Isaiah 62:6
[5] Ephesians 6:18-19

[6] Colossians 4:2-3
[7] John 16:24
[8] Compare Matthew 7:8 and John 16:24.
[9] Romans 8:26
[10] 1 Thessalonians 5:16-18
[11] Revelation 4:8

PERSONAL NOTES

_____

_____

_____

_____

_____

_____

_____

_____

_____

INDEX

C

D

E

F

G

J

K

L

P

R

S

W

Y